Bridging Sustainability: Empowering Business Through ESG & First Nations Partnerships

Introduction:

In today's rapidly evolving world, businesses face an unprecedented challenge: balancing profitability with responsibility. As environmental, social, and governance (ESG) principles increasingly shape the global business landscape, organisations are called upon to not only drive growth but to contribute to the well-being of our planet and its people. One of the most powerful ways to achieve this is through a holistic approach that embraces sustainability, fosters biodiversity, and actively engages with Indigenous communities.

This book explores the vital intersection of ESG practices, biodiversity conservation, and First Nations empowerment in Australia. We delve into how businesses can incorporate Indigenous knowledge, respect land rights, and support the custodians of Australia's natural environments while aligning their operations with sustainability goals. Through real-world examples, actionable strategies, and deep insights into collaborative partnerships, this work offers a roadmap for businesses that are committed to being part of the solution.

As we move forward, the need for inclusive, ethical, and sustainable practices has never been more critical. It is not enough to merely meet the demands of today; we must think ahead, ensuring that the way we operate today lays the foundation for a better tomorrow. Join us on this journey as we explore how businesses can support biodiversity, promote environmental stewardship, and strengthen relationships with First Nations communities in Australia, all while building a resilient and sustainable future for all.

Table of Contents

Chapter 1: Introduction to ESG, Biodiversity, and First Nations Communities in Australia
Chapter 2: Exploring Indigenous Ecological Knowledge and Its Role in Biodiversity Conservation
Chapter 3: Exploring the Role of First Nations in ESG Frameworks
Chapter 4: Navigating the Intersection of Corporate Responsibility and Indigenous Sovereignty
Chapter 5: Case Studies of Successful Business-First Nations Partnerships
Chapter 6: Global Perspectives on ESG and Indigenous Partnerships
Chapter 7: Implementing Global Best Practices in Australia: ESG, Biodiversity, and First Nations
Chapter 8: Government Policy and the Role of Public Institutions in Supporting ESG and First Nations Partnerships
Chapter 9: Engaging First Nations Communities in ESG Initiatives
Chapter 10: Implementing Accountability and Transparency in ESG Initiatives with First Nations
Chapter 11: Building a Culture of Sustainability Within the Organization
Chapter 12: Innovation and Technology Driving Sustainability
Chapter 13: Monitoring, Measuring, and Reporting Sustainability Progress
Chapter 14: Building Resilient and Adaptive Sustainability Strategies
Chapter 15: Communicating Sustainability and Resilience to Stakeholders
Chapter 16: The Future of Sustainability: Emerging Trends and Innovations
Chapter 17: Leadership for Sustainability: Driving Change from the Top
Chapter 18: Integrating ESG and Biodiversity into Business Strategies
Chapter 19: Engaging Stakeholders in Biodiversity and ESG Efforts
Chapter 20: Measuring and Reporting the Impact of Biodiversity Initiatives
Chapter 21: The Role of Technology in Biodiversity Monitoring and Sustainability Tools
Chapter 22: Integrating First Nations Knowledge in Biodiversity Conservation
Chapter 23: Contributing to the Sustainable Development Goals (SDGs) Through ESG Strategies

Chapter 1: Introduction to ESG, Biodiversity, and First Nations Communities in Australia

1.1 Understanding ESG in the Modern Context

Environmental, Social, and Governance (ESG) is a framework that organisations use to assess and manage their impact on society and the environment. In recent years, ESG has gained significant traction as businesses, governments, and non-governmental organisations (NGOs) increasingly recognise the importance of sustainable practices. ESG criteria help stakeholders, including investors and consumers, understand how a company or organisation performs in three key areas:

- **Environmental:** How a company manages its environmental impact, including emissions, resource consumption, waste management, and efforts to promote sustainability.

- **Social:** This aspect focuses on relationships with stakeholders, including employees, suppliers, customers, and communities. It encompasses workplace diversity, community engagement, and human rights issues.

- **Governance:** The structures and practices that determine how a company is run. It involves the transparency of decision-making processes, ethical behaviour, and accountability to stakeholders.

1.2 The Role of Biodiversity in ESG

Biodiversity refers to the variety of life on Earth, from ecosystems to species and genetic diversity. In the context of ESG, biodiversity plays a critical role in environmental sustainability. Biodiversity loss can lead to ecological imbalances, threatening the health of ecosystems that many industries rely on for resources, stability, and productivity.

Protecting biodiversity is crucial for achieving long-term sustainability goals, as it supports ecosystem services such as clean water, food production, and carbon sequestration. These services are essential for the global economy and human well-being. Integrating biodiversity into ESG strategies has thus become an imperative for businesses aiming to reduce their environmental impact and maintain a harmonious relationship with the natural world.

Incorporating biodiversity into corporate strategies can be challenging due to the complex interdependencies of ecosystems.

However, by understanding the interconnectedness of biodiversity with other aspects of the environment, companies can develop strategies that support biodiversity conservation while also pursuing their own sustainability objectives.

1.3 The Connection Between First Nations Communities and ESG

First Nations communities in Australia have a deep connection to the land, water, and natural resources. Indigenous Australians have been stewards of their land for tens of thousands of years, practicing sustainable land management techniques and caring for biodiversity through traditional ecological knowledge (TEK). First Nations knowledge is based on a holistic understanding of nature and its cycles, deeply embedded in culture, spirituality, and community practices.

In recent years, there has been growing recognition of the need to integrate First Nations perspectives into contemporary governance, environmental practices, and economic models, particularly in the context of ESG. This is a step towards recognising the sovereignty and rights of Indigenous communities, which includes their right to self-determination in environmental decision-making.

As the global focus shifts towards more sustainable practices, businesses, governments, and NGOs have begun to engage more with First Nations communities, acknowledging their knowledge and leadership in conservation and sustainable land management practices. This is not only a form of reconciliation but also an opportunity for businesses to align their operations with the long-term sustainability that Indigenous knowledge provides.

1.4 Why ESG and Biodiversity Matter for First Nations Communities

Biodiversity is integral to the cultural identity, health, and livelihood of many First Nations communities. Land and water are central to their traditions, spirituality, and sustenance, making biodiversity conservation a deeply personal matter. Indigenous communities have unique insights into biodiversity and ecosystems due to their long-standing relationship with the land.

However, the exploitation of natural resources, climate change, and unsustainable land-use practices have placed considerable pressure on the biodiversity that these communities rely on. Many First Nations communities have been at the forefront of advocating for the protection of ecosystems, yet their voices are often sidelined in broader discussions around conservation and environmental policy.

1.5 The Need for Collaboration: First Nations, Business, and Government

Achieving the Sustainable Development Goals (SDGs) and the broader objectives of ESG requires collaboration across sectors. First Nations communities must be seen as partners in biodiversity conservation, not just stakeholders to consult or work with occasionally. For a truly sustainable and inclusive approach to ESG, businesses and governments must work alongside Indigenous leaders to develop policies and practices that reflect both traditional knowledge and contemporary science.

This partnership approach can lead to more effective conservation strategies, as traditional ecological knowledge offers valuable insights into land management, biodiversity protection, and climate resilience. Collaborative initiatives can result in policies that support both the protection of the environment and the social and economic empowerment of First Nations communities.

1.6 Looking Ahead

This chapter has set the stage for understanding how ESG principles intersect with biodiversity conservation and the vital role First Nations communities play in these efforts. As the book progresses, we will delve deeper into the individual components of ESG in the context of biodiversity and First Nations, exploring practical strategies, case studies, and future opportunities for collaboration.

We will explore how businesses can meaningfully integrate First Nations knowledge into their sustainability practices and the ways in which they can support biodiversity conservation through partnerships. In the following chapters, we will also address the challenges that businesses, governments, and communities face in aligning ESG goals with Indigenous rights and the protection of biodiversity.

Chapter 2: Exploring Indigenous Ecological Knowledge and Its Role in Biodiversity Conservation

2.1 Understanding Indigenous Ecological Knowledge (IEK)

Indigenous Ecological Knowledge (IEK), also referred to as Traditional Ecological Knowledge (TEK), is the cumulative body of knowledge, practices, and beliefs developed over millennia by Indigenous peoples. It encompasses an understanding of ecosystems, species, and environmental processes passed down through generations. IEK is not just a scientific body of knowledge, but is deeply integrated with spiritual beliefs, cultural values, and traditional practices.

In Australia, Aboriginal and Torres Strait Islander communities have maintained a profound connection to the land, water, and sea, using sustainable land management practices that promote the health of ecosystems. This knowledge is both practical and philosophical. It involves understanding the seasonal patterns of plants and animals, knowing how to care for and restore the land, and applying rituals that ensure balance with nature.

2.2 The Link Between IEK and Biodiversity Conservation

Indigenous knowledge systems have long demonstrated an intrinsic understanding of biodiversity conservation. For example, Indigenous fire management practices—such as cool burns—have been used for thousands of years to reduce the risk of larger wildfires and maintain the health of forests and grasslands. These practices were developed based on a detailed understanding of local ecosystems and animal behaviour.

Similarly, First Nations peoples have cultivated knowledge about the sustainable harvesting of marine and terrestrial resources. Through practices such as rotational harvesting, the use of sacred sites, and the conservation of waterholes and wetlands, they ensured that the biodiversity of these areas remained intact over long periods of time.

What's critical about IEK in the context of biodiversity is its holistic approach. Unlike Western environmental practices, which often treat land and species management in isolated contexts, Indigenous knowledge incorporates the interconnectedness of species, ecosystems, and human society. This understanding has helped Indigenous communities maintain biodiversity in some of the most biologically rich regions of the world, including Australia.

2.3 The Value of Indigenous Knowledge in Modern Conservation Practices

The integration of IEK with modern conservation science can provide a more nuanced approach to environmental stewardship. In recent years, environmental organisations, researchers, and governments have started to recognise the importance of blending traditional knowledge with contemporary scientific methods. This partnership approach can address the gaps left by traditional conservation methods and offer solutions that are not only ecologically effective but also socially inclusive.

For example, Indigenous communities across Australia are working with governmental and non-governmental organisations to restore degraded landscapes, protect endangered species, and manage natural resources in ways that benefit both the environment and the community. These efforts integrate modern technology with Indigenous practices such as firestick alliances, seasonal hunting practices, and water management, creating a more comprehensive conservation strategy.

2.4 Successful Examples of IEK in Biodiversity Conservation

There are numerous examples of Indigenous knowledge being successfully integrated into conservation efforts across Australia. One notable example is the work of the **Gunditjmara people** in the **Budj Bim National Heritage Landscape** in Victoria. The Gunditjmara people developed an extensive system of aquaculture, managing wetlands and waterways for thousands of years to trap and farm eels. This sophisticated system, which was recently recognised as a UNESCO World Heritage site, has proven to be an effective method for biodiversity preservation.

In the **Kimberley region** of Western Australia, Indigenous rangers are using traditional knowledge alongside scientific research to conserve marine environments. By implementing culturally informed management practices, the **Wunambal Gaambera people** have helped to protect critical turtle nesting sites and marine biodiversity while fostering sustainable fisheries.

In these cases, IEK provides a foundation for modern conservation initiatives. It offers a culturally relevant, effective, and ecologically harmonious approach to managing Australia's rich biodiversity.

2.5 The Challenges in Integrating IEK into Modern Conservation Frameworks

Despite the successes, integrating Indigenous knowledge into mainstream biodiversity conservation practices can be challenging. For centuries, Indigenous knowledge systems have been marginalised, with Western scientific models often treating traditional knowledge as anecdotal or inferior. This historical disconnect has created barriers to collaboration and has limited the inclusion of First Nations perspectives in policy-making.

Further complicating the situation is the issue of **intellectual property** and **cultural heritage**. Many Indigenous knowledge systems are sacred and inherently tied to cultural identity. This raises ethical questions about how traditional knowledge is used and shared, especially in contexts where businesses or governments may seek to commercialise or exploit it.

Additionally, for partnerships between Indigenous communities and conservation organisations to be effective, there needs to be mutual trust and respect. Indigenous communities must have control over how their knowledge is utilised, ensuring that it is applied in ways that benefit both the environment and their cultural values.

2.6 Moving Forward: Best Practices for Integrating IEK into Biodiversity Conservation

The future of biodiversity conservation relies on creating more opportunities for collaboration between Indigenous peoples and conservation practitioners. Here are some best practices for successfully integrating Indigenous Ecological Knowledge into modern conservation frameworks:

- **Co-Management and Co-Governance:** Engaging Indigenous communities in co-management roles, ensuring that they have a voice in the governance of protected areas and conservation initiatives. This helps ensure that conservation efforts are culturally appropriate and scientifically effective.

- **Capacity-Building:** Investing in training programs for both Indigenous rangers and conservation scientists to ensure that both knowledge systems are respected and effectively utilised. Capacity-building can help empower Indigenous communities to take leadership roles in biodiversity conservation.

- **Respect for Intellectual Property:** Developing frameworks that respect the intellectual property rights of

Indigenous peoples, ensuring that their traditional knowledge is used ethically and with consent. This can involve agreements on benefit-sharing and recognition of Indigenous intellectual property in conservation projects.

- **Community-Led Conservation Projects:** Encouraging the establishment of conservation projects led by Indigenous communities that draw on their traditional knowledge and skills. This can be paired with funding and resources from government or non-governmental organisations to ensure that these projects are both effective and sustainable.

2.7 The Future of Biodiversity Conservation: A Collaborative Path Forward

Incorporating Indigenous knowledge into modern conservation strategies not only benefits biodiversity but also strengthens the relationship between Indigenous communities and the broader public. These collaborations support a vision of conservation that is inclusive, respects the rights of Indigenous peoples, and recognises their role as the stewards of the land.

As the world continues to face challenges related to climate change, habitat destruction, and biodiversity loss, the integration of IEK with contemporary conservation practices offers a solution that is both innovative and deeply rooted in the wisdom of the land. By respecting and valuing this knowledge, we create a future where both the environment and Indigenous cultures can thrive together.

Chapter 3: Exploring the Role of First Nations in ESG Frameworks

3.1 Understanding ESG and Its Relevance to First Nations

Environmental, Social, and Governance (ESG) frameworks have gained significant traction over the past few decades as tools for evaluating and driving business responsibility in a rapidly changing world. ESG frameworks provide organisations with a structured approach to managing sustainability, social justice, and corporate governance while mitigating risks associated with climate change, social inequality, and poor governance.

First Nations communities, with their profound connection to the land and deep-rooted traditions of stewardship, are increasingly recognised as key partners in the achievement of global sustainability goals, including the United Nations' Sustainable Development Goals (SDGs). Their participation in ESG frameworks is not only vital for protecting the environment but also for ensuring that the social and governance aspects of sustainability are genuinely inclusive and equitable.

Integrating First Nations knowledge and practices into ESG frameworks offers a unique opportunity to amplify the effectiveness of environmental management, promote social equity, and build stronger governance systems that honor Indigenous sovereignty and rights. These frameworks must reflect Indigenous values, and it's essential for businesses to ensure that their operations align with the principles of self-determination, cultural preservation, and environmental sustainability.

3.2 The Environmental Dimension: Leveraging Traditional Knowledge for Sustainable Management

First Nations communities possess a wealth of traditional ecological knowledge (TEK), which has been accumulated over thousands of years. This knowledge has been passed down through generations, grounded in an intimate understanding of local ecosystems, biodiversity, and natural cycles. For businesses looking to engage with sustainability practices, incorporating TEK into their environmental strategies is a powerful tool for enhancing biodiversity protection, reducing ecological footprints, and promoting long-term environmental stewardship.

Key Areas of Integration:

- **Land and Fire Management:** Indigenous fire practices, such as **cool burns**, are used to prevent large-scale wildfires and maintain the health of specific ecosystems. By partnering with Indigenous communities, businesses can integrate these traditional fire management techniques into their land-use planning to reduce fire risks and protect native flora and fauna.

- **Water Management:** Many First Nations peoples have sustainable water practices that ensure the long-term health of freshwater and marine ecosystems. These practices can inform water use policies, helping businesses mitigate the risks of water scarcity and contamination.

- **Biodiversity Conservation:** First Nations' land management practices ensure the preservation of diverse habitats. Indigenous knowledge of rotational harvesting, sustainable fishing, and responsible land use has proven to be highly effective in maintaining ecosystem balance, preventing overharvesting, and ensuring biodiversity remains intact.

By including First Nations perspectives on land management and biodiversity conservation within ESG frameworks, companies can significantly enhance the sustainability of their operations, especially in environments rich in natural resources.

3.3 The Social Dimension: Empowering Indigenous Communities and Promoting Social Equity

One of the fundamental pillars of ESG is the social aspect, which focuses on the well-being of communities, equality, and inclusivity. For businesses, aligning with social responsibility entails addressing the needs of marginalised communities, promoting diversity, and fostering community development.

First Nations communities are often disproportionately affected by social challenges such as poverty, inadequate access to healthcare, and discrimination. Addressing these challenges is an essential part of any robust ESG strategy. Companies can play a pivotal role in supporting First Nations communities by prioritising Indigenous employment opportunities, developing community-focused projects, and engaging in initiatives that promote social justice and equity.

Key Areas of Integration:

- **Employment and Training:** By actively involving Indigenous peoples in the workforce, businesses can provide valuable job opportunities and skills development, especially in leadership roles. This helps foster economic empowerment and reduces unemployment rates within First Nations communities.

- **Cultural Inclusion:** Businesses should adopt policies that promote the inclusion of First Nations culture, language, and heritage within the workplace. This might involve creating spaces for cultural expression, ensuring cultural safety, and recognising the importance of traditional knowledge in business operations.

- **Community Engagement:** Businesses must engage with First Nations communities to understand their specific needs and priorities. This can include participating in consultations, funding community-driven projects, and ensuring that community voices are heard in decision-making processes.

Incorporating social justice principles into ESG strategies ensures that businesses contribute to a more inclusive and equitable society, where Indigenous rights and perspectives are acknowledged and respected.

3.4 The Governance Dimension: Embedding Indigenous Rights and Self-Determination

Governance in ESG refers to the structures, processes, and behaviors that guide a company's decision-making, leadership, and accountability. Effective governance includes compliance with laws, ethical conduct, and transparency, all of which are vital to long-term business success. However, effective governance also entails recognising and respecting the rights of Indigenous peoples, their sovereignty, and their role as stewards of the land.

For businesses that wish to align their operations with ESG best practices, it is critical to include First Nations communities in governance processes. This means respecting their land rights, ensuring their participation in decision-making, and providing opportunities for self-determination.

Key Areas of Integration:

- **Respecting Land Rights and Sovereignty:** Indigenous communities hold unique rights to their ancestral lands. Businesses must engage in ethical land agreements, respecting First Nations' sovereignty and rights, especially in resource-extractive industries like mining, agriculture, and forestry.

- **Co-Governance Structures:** Co-governance is a model where businesses, governments, and Indigenous peoples collaborate in managing land and natural resources. By adopting co-governance frameworks, businesses ensure that First Nations communities have a say in the management of their traditional territories and contribute to decision-making processes.

- **Transparency and Accountability:** Embedding transparency into business operations means ensuring that First Nations communities are kept informed about business activities and their potential impacts on the land and people. Reporting on ESG performance in a manner that acknowledges and integrates Indigenous knowledge and rights promotes trust and ensures accountability.

3.5 Best Practices for Integrating First Nations Perspectives into ESG Frameworks

For businesses aiming to integrate First Nations knowledge, rights, and perspectives into their ESG frameworks, here are several best practices to ensure a collaborative, respectful, and effective approach:

- **Consultation and Consent:** Prioritise consultation with First Nations communities through structured and meaningful engagement processes. Secure Free, Prior, and Informed Consent (FPIC) before starting any projects that may impact their lands or resources.

- **Long-Term Partnerships:** Foster long-term, trust-based partnerships with Indigenous communities rather than short-term project-based collaborations. This approach ensures the integration of Indigenous priorities and sustainability objectives into business strategies.

- **Cultural Awareness Training:** Offer training programs to staff and leadership on the history, values, and rights of First Nations peoples. This education promotes respectful relationships and ensures that business operations are culturally sensitive.

- **Support Indigenous-Led Projects:** Invest in projects and initiatives that are led and driven by Indigenous peoples. This can range from environmental conservation to cultural education programs, ensuring that First Nations communities are at the forefront of their own development and environmental stewardship.

- **Align ESG Goals with Indigenous Rights:** Ensure that the business's ESG goals align with and support Indigenous rights, including self-determination, cultural preservation, and access to land and resources.

3.6 Conclusion: A Path Toward a Collaborative and Sustainable Future

The integration of First Nations perspectives into ESG frameworks is not just a moral or legal obligation—it is an essential step toward creating a sustainable and equitable future for all. Businesses that embrace this integration not only foster stronger relationships with Indigenous communities but also contribute to the global movement toward sustainability, equity, and responsible governance.

By recognising and valuing Indigenous knowledge, practices, and rights, businesses can play a pivotal role in driving positive change, ensuring that both people and the planet thrive for generations to come.

Chapter 4: Navigating the Intersection of Corporate Responsibility and Indigenous Sovereignty

4.1 Understanding Indigenous Sovereignty and Corporate Responsibility

Indigenous sovereignty refers to the right of Indigenous peoples to govern themselves and manage their traditional lands and resources according to their own cultural practices, laws, and priorities. It is a fundamental principle that underpins the relationship between Indigenous communities and external entities, such as businesses and governments. Respecting Indigenous sovereignty is essential for fostering a partnership that honors the rights of First Nations peoples and promotes sustainable development.

Corporate responsibility, in this context, goes beyond simply meeting legal requirements or adhering to ethical business practices. It involves recognising and engaging with the rights of Indigenous peoples as stewards of the land, supporting their autonomy, and ensuring that their participation in decision-making is central to any business activities on their territories. The intersection of corporate responsibility and Indigenous sovereignty is crucial for the success of sustainable development initiatives, particularly in sectors that impact the environment, such as mining, forestry, energy, and agriculture.

Businesses operating in areas with significant Indigenous populations must develop governance frameworks that respect Indigenous laws, customs, and decision-making structures. Doing so is not only legally and morally sound, but it also presents opportunities to build mutually beneficial relationships that can drive long-term success.

4.2 Legal and Ethical Foundations of Indigenous Sovereignty

The foundation for respecting Indigenous sovereignty in business operations is built on both legal principles and ethical standards. In many countries, legal frameworks such as the United Nations Declaration on the Rights of Indigenous Peoples (UNDRIP) provide international guidelines on the rights of Indigenous peoples, including the right to self-determination, cultural preservation, and land use. These frameworks serve as a crucial reference for businesses seeking to engage with Indigenous communities in a respectful and legally compliant manner.

UNDRIP and Corporate Responsibility:

- **Article 19** of UNDRIP states that Indigenous peoples have the right to be consulted and involved in decision-making processes that affect their lands, territories, and resources.

- **Article 32** emphasizes the right of Indigenous peoples to give or withhold their free, prior, and informed consent (FPIC) before the initiation of projects that may affect their lands or resources.

For businesses, this means that any operation or development within Indigenous territories should involve active, transparent engagement with First Nations communities from the outset. Obtaining FPIC is a critical step in aligning with both international human rights standards and responsible corporate practices.

However, businesses must go beyond legal obligations and aim for an ethical approach. Ethical responsibility entails understanding and respecting the deeper cultural values and governance systems of Indigenous peoples, not merely fulfilling legal requirements. This requires businesses to approach partnerships with humility, listening to the voices of Indigenous leaders, and incorporating their views and aspirations into business plans and decisions.

4.3 Best Practices for Integrating Indigenous Sovereignty into Business Operations

Integrating Indigenous sovereignty into business operations involves a series of practices designed to foster respect, collaboration, and co-ownership. These best practices reflect a commitment to reconciliation, responsible development, and long-term partnership building.

1. Engaging in Meaningful Consultation and Consent

Before embarking on any projects that affect Indigenous lands or resources, businesses must Prioritise consultation with Indigenous communities. The goal is to not only seek consent but to engage in an ongoing dialogue that acknowledges the community's right to self-determination. Consultation should be free, prior, and informed (FPIC), and conducted in a culturally appropriate manner that respects Indigenous knowledge systems.

Key Actions:

- Schedule community meetings and consultations that include traditional leaders, Elders, and other relevant community members.

- Develop clear, accessible documentation that explains the project's potential impacts and benefits.

- Provide resources and support to help communities engage in the decision-making process.

By ensuring that Indigenous communities are actively involved and have the final say in matters affecting their lands, businesses demonstrate a commitment to their rights and strengthen their relationship with the community.

2. Respecting Indigenous Governance Systems

Every Indigenous community has its own system of governance, which is based on cultural values, laws, and customs. These governance systems often differ significantly from Western models, which can lead to misunderstandings or conflicts if not approached with respect. Businesses must make a concerted effort to learn about and engage with Indigenous governance structures and decision-making processes.

Key Actions:

- Recognise the role of traditional leaders and local governance bodies in decisions related to land, resources, and community welfare.

- Ensure that agreements and partnerships with Indigenous communities align with their governance structures.

- Integrate Indigenous perspectives into strategic planning and decision-making processes.

Respecting Indigenous governance means allowing communities to lead their own development and ensuring their values are upheld in all business interactions.

3. Supporting Community-Led Development Initiatives

A key aspect of respecting Indigenous sovereignty is supporting community-driven development. Businesses can play a significant role in empowering First Nations communities by providing funding, resources, and technical assistance for initiatives that reflect the needs and aspirations of the community. This may include education programs, health initiatives, sustainable land management practices, and renewable energy projects.

Key Actions:

- Work with Indigenous communities to identify areas where business involvement can create positive social impact.

- Provide funding for projects that align with the community's goals, such as cultural preservation, education, and environmental sustainability.

- Ensure that the benefits of these initiatives remain within the community, helping to create long-term economic empowerment.

Supporting community-led development initiatives not only contributes to the well-being of Indigenous communities but also strengthens the overall sustainability of business operations.

4.4 Building Trust and Ensuring Long-Term Engagement

Establishing trust with Indigenous communities is a gradual process that requires long-term commitment. Businesses must recognise that relationships with First Nations peoples are built on respect, transparency, and mutual understanding. The key to success lies in maintaining continuous and genuine engagement, demonstrating respect for cultural heritage, and ensuring that the community's interests are Prioritised.

Key Actions:

- Develop long-term partnerships with First Nations communities, rather than focusing on short-term projects.

- Regularly update Indigenous partners on the progress of initiatives and address any concerns that arise.

- Create opportunities for Indigenous people to take leadership roles within business operations, ensuring their voices are heard and valued.

Long-term engagement involves acknowledging the historical and contemporary challenges faced by Indigenous communities and working in partnership to create positive change that is mutually beneficial.

4.5 Conclusion: Respecting Sovereignty for a Shared Future

The intersection of corporate responsibility and Indigenous sovereignty presents both challenges and opportunities for businesses. By respecting Indigenous rights and governance, businesses can build sustainable, ethical partnerships that contribute to the well-being of First Nations communities and the environment. This requires not just compliance with legal frameworks like UNDRIP but a deeper commitment to embedding Indigenous perspectives into business strategy and operations.

As businesses work toward achieving environmental and social goals, they must recognise that the path to sustainable development and reconciliation is one of collaboration, mutual respect, and shared responsibility. Only by respecting the sovereignty of Indigenous peoples and their connection to the land can businesses create lasting, positive change that benefits both their operations and the communities they work with.

Chapter 5: Case Studies of Successful Business-First Nations Partnerships

In this chapter, we explore several case studies where businesses have successfully integrated First Nations perspectives into their environmental, social, and governance (ESG) strategies. These examples highlight the potential for businesses to foster long-term partnerships with Indigenous communities, ensuring both economic and environmental sustainability while respecting cultural heritage and sovereignty. The goal is to demonstrate how businesses can navigate complex relationships with First Nations communities and build mutually beneficial outcomes that contribute to shared goals of sustainability, resilience, and economic development.

5.1 Case Study 1: BHP and the Yinhawangka People – A Partnership for Sustainable Mining

Background: BHP, one of the world's largest mining companies, operates across various sectors, including iron ore, copper, and energy. The company has long had a presence in Australia, and as its operations expanded, it engaged with Indigenous communities across the country to ensure their involvement in decision-making processes. One notable example is the partnership between BHP and the Yinhawangka people, traditional landowners of the area around the Mount Whaleback mine in Western Australia.

Key Actions:

- **Cultural Heritage Protection:** In this partnership, BHP worked closely with the Yinhawangka people to protect their cultural heritage sites while mining. BHP implemented environmental protection measures based on the Yinhawangka community's knowledge and traditions, ensuring that sacred sites were not disturbed by mining activities.

- **Co-Management of Land:** BHP and the Yinhawangka people co-manage large areas of land. The Yinhawangka people were involved in the environmental assessments of new mining sites and were consulted on land use decisions, ensuring that their sovereignty was respected and their cultural practices were integrated into land management strategies.

- **Capacity Building:** The partnership also involved capacity-building initiatives, including training programs for Yinhawangka people in areas like land management, environmental monitoring, and even roles within the mining company itself. This approach aimed to build skills that would allow community members to actively participate in decision-making and economic activities.

Outcomes:

- **Environmental Sustainability:** By respecting cultural heritage and integrating traditional ecological knowledge, BHP's mining operations were more environmentally sustainable, with less disruption to the surrounding ecosystems.

- **Economic Empowerment:** The community benefited economically through employment and business opportunities. The partnership also helped create a framework for future collaborative efforts with other Indigenous communities.

- **Stronger Relationships:** Through ongoing dialogue and collaboration, BHP has built a trusted relationship with the Yinhawangka people, which has extended beyond mining operations and into broader social initiatives, fostering positive social outcomes for the community.

5.2 Case Study 2: Rio Tinto and the Traditional Owners of the Pilbara – Collaborative Environmental Stewardship

Background: Rio Tinto, a global mining company, has a long history of working with Indigenous communities in Australia. One of the most significant partnerships is with the traditional owners of the Pilbara region, home to Rio Tinto's iron ore operations. The collaboration focuses on ensuring the environmental sustainability of mining practices while respecting and enhancing the cultural heritage of the Indigenous communities.

Key Actions:

- **Environmental and Cultural Consultations:** Rio Tinto engages in regular consultations with the traditional owners, ensuring that their concerns are heard and that their perspectives are incorporated into the company's environmental strategies. This includes setting up community advisory boards and regular feedback sessions on the environmental impact of operations.

- **Shared Environmental Monitoring:** As part of its partnership with the traditional owners, Rio Tinto has shared environmental monitoring responsibilities. This involves the traditional owners actively participating in tracking and assessing the impacts of mining on local ecosystems, particularly around water sources and biodiversity.

- **Protecting Sacred Sites:** Rio Tinto has committed to protecting sacred sites in the Pilbara region. Through collaboration with the traditional owners, the company has avoided mining operations in sensitive cultural areas. These efforts align with the Indigenous peoples' cultural rights and Rio Tinto's corporate commitment to sustainable and responsible resource extraction.

Outcomes:

- **Enhanced Environmental Protection:** By integrating the knowledge of traditional owners into its environmental practices, Rio Tinto has been able to mitigate the environmental impact of its mining activities. The collaborative environmental monitoring program has provided valuable insights into how to better manage the local ecosystems and water resources.

- **Cultural Preservation:** The partnership ensured that sacred Indigenous sites were preserved and that mining operations were conducted in a way that minimized cultural disruption. This reflects Rio Tinto's growing commitment to responsible operations in Indigenous territories.

- **Strengthened Community Relations:** The ongoing partnership and commitment to shared environmental goals have strengthened relations between Rio Tinto and the traditional owners. The engagement has also opened doors for future collaborative projects, such as cultural heritage preservation and community development.

5.3 Case Study 3: AGL Energy and the Gunditjmara People – Renewable Energy and Economic Empowerment

Background: AGL Energy, one of Australia's largest energy companies, partnered with the Gunditjmara people to develop a renewable energy project. The Gunditjmara people are the traditional owners of land near Lake Condah in Western Victoria, an area known for its cultural significance and ancient aquaculture systems. The Gunditjmara people are also recognised for their strong connection to the land and their leadership in advocating for sustainable energy solutions.

Key Actions:

- **Renewable Energy Development:** AGL worked closely with the Gunditjmara people to develop a renewable energy project that would generate clean energy for the region. This involved using sustainable energy technologies, including wind and solar power, while ensuring that the development adhered to traditional land use practices and protected the Gunditjmara people's cultural heritage.

- **Economic Partnerships:** A key component of the partnership was creating economic opportunities for the Gunditjmara people through participation in the energy sector. The project provided jobs and business opportunities for the local community, including the provision of services and construction of renewable energy infrastructure.

- **Cultural Heritage Preservation:** The development of the renewable energy project was conducted in parallel with efforts to preserve the Gunditjmara people's cultural heritage. AGL worked with the Gunditjmara community to ensure that their sacred and historical sites, particularly those associated with their ancient aquaculture systems, were protected from any adverse impacts from the project.

Outcomes:

- **Environmental Sustainability:** The project successfully contributed to Australia's transition to renewable energy, reducing the region's reliance on fossil fuels while supporting the Gunditjmara people's values of sustainability.

- **Community Empowerment:** The Gunditjmara people benefited economically through their involvement in the renewable energy project, enhancing their financial independence and providing new avenues for local development.

- **Cultural and Environmental Integration:** The careful integration of cultural preservation with environmental sustainability ensured that the Gunditjmara people's traditions were honored while fostering economic growth and clean energy solutions.

5.4 Case Study 4: Telstra and the Aboriginal Land Councils – Connectivity and Digital Empowerment

Background: Telstra, Australia's largest telecommunications company, has engaged with Aboriginal Land Councils across the country to improve digital access and connectivity in remote Indigenous communities. This initiative aims to bridge the digital divide by providing improved communication services while respecting the needs and rights of Indigenous peoples.

Key Actions:

- **Infrastructure Development:** Telstra worked with Aboriginal Land Councils to build telecommunications infrastructure in remote areas, ensuring that Indigenous communities had access to reliable internet and mobile services.

- **Community Consultation:** Throughout the planning and implementation of these projects, Telstra maintained open dialogue with local Indigenous leaders and communities, ensuring that their needs were central to the development process.

- **Digital Literacy Programs:** Telstra partnered with local Indigenous organisations to provide digital literacy training, enabling community members to use new technologies effectively for education, healthcare, and business development.

Outcomes:

- **Increased Access to Technology:** The project significantly increased access to digital services in remote

Indigenous communities, contributing to greater social and economic inclusion.

- **Economic Opportunities:** By improving connectivity, Telstra has enabled Indigenous businesses to thrive and has helped reduce isolation in rural and remote areas, fostering economic growth.

- **Empowerment and Capacity Building:** The digital literacy programs have empowered local communities, providing essential skills that can be used for personal, professional, and communal growth.

5.5 Conclusion: Lessons Learned and Pathways Forward

These case studies illustrate the importance of collaboration and mutual respect in business-Indigenous partnerships. The lessons learned from these examples include the critical need for businesses to engage deeply with Indigenous communities, to respect their governance structures, and to align projects with their cultural values and aspirations. By doing so, businesses can create long-lasting, positive impacts that benefit both their operations and the communities they work with.

As businesses continue to recognise the importance of ESG principles, they must remain committed to integrating Indigenous perspectives into their strategies. This not only helps protect and preserve Indigenous cultures but also contributes to global sustainability efforts and the achievement of the United Nations' Sustainable Development Goals.

Chapter 6: Global Perspectives on ESG and Indigenous Partnerships

In this chapter, we explore how businesses around the world have successfully integrated ESG principles into their operations while collaborating with Indigenous communities. We will look at international case studies that offer insights into how companies can strengthen their commitment to sustainability, respect for Indigenous rights, and cultural sensitivity. By examining these examples, we aim to provide a broader context for how businesses in Australia can further enhance their engagement with First Nations communities while contributing to the achievement of global ESG and sustainability goals.

6.1 Case Study 1: Newmont Mining and the Navajo Nation – Indigenous Land Stewardship and Mining

Background: Newmont Mining, a major gold mining company, has long been involved in a partnership with the Navajo Nation in the southwestern United States. The Navajo Nation holds one of the largest reservations in the U.S., spanning parts of Arizona, Utah, and New Mexico. Over the years, Newmont has worked with the Navajo Nation to address environmental concerns related to mining operations and to ensure the community benefits from mining activities.

Key Actions:

- **Environmental Stewardship:** Newmont Mining works closely with the Navajo Nation to ensure that mining activities do not harm sacred land or natural resources. The company has implemented several environmental protection measures, such as water conservation practices, reclamation of mining sites, and the use of sustainable mining technologies to reduce environmental impact.

- **Cultural Sensitivity:** Newmont recognises the cultural significance of the land to the Navajo people. As part of their partnership, the company consulted with Navajo leaders and community members to ensure that all mining activities were aligned with the cultural values of the community.

- **Revenue Sharing and Economic Development:** Newmont has committed to revenue-sharing agreements that benefit the Navajo Nation. These agreements include financial compensation for land use and investments in infrastructure projects that support the community, such as education and healthcare facilities.

Outcomes:

- **Environmental Protection:** Through close consultation with the Navajo Nation, Newmont has been able to implement mining practices that minimize harm to the environment and protect sacred sites.

- **Cultural and Community Benefits:** The Navajo Nation has seen increased economic benefits from the partnership, with job opportunities and infrastructure development supporting long-term community resilience.

- **Positive Reputation and Social License to Operate:** By prioritising cultural sensitivity and environmental stewardship, Newmont has strengthened its social license to operate, building trust with the Navajo Nation and the wider public.

6.2 Case Study 2: IKEA and the Sami People – Sustainable Forestry and Traditional Knowledge

Background: IKEA, the global furniture retailer, has made significant strides in aligning its operations with sustainable practices. One of its key sustainability initiatives involves sourcing wood from responsible forestry operations, and a notable collaboration has taken place with the Sami people of Scandinavia. The Sami are an Indigenous group whose traditional lands stretch across Norway, Sweden, Finland, and Russia, and they have long been stewards of the forests in the region.

Key Actions:

- **Sustainable Forestry Practices:** IKEA partnered with the Sami people to implement sustainable forestry practices that respect both the environment and the rights of the Sami. IKEA worked with the Sami to incorporate traditional knowledge into modern forestry techniques, ensuring that logging activities did not disrupt the natural balance of the forests or encroach upon areas of cultural significance.

- **Certification of Forests:** IKEA collaborated with the Forest Stewardship Council (FSC) and other certification bodies to ensure that forests were managed according to the highest environmental and social standards. The Sami people played a role in ensuring that forestry practices were not only environmentally sustainable but also culturally appropriate.

- **Economic Benefits for the Sami People:** IKEA's partnership with the Sami people also included providing them with economic benefits from their participation in sustainable forestry operations. This partnership enabled the Sami to continue their traditional way of life while engaging in modern business practices.

Outcomes:

- **Environmental Sustainability:** By integrating traditional knowledge into forestry practices, IKEA was able to reduce its environmental footprint while ensuring that the forests were managed sustainably for future generations.

- **Cultural Preservation:** The collaboration ensured that Sami cultural values were preserved, including the protection of sacred lands and the integration of traditional ecological knowledge into land management.

- **Economic Empowerment:** The Sami people benefited economically through their involvement in the forestry industry, which helped diversify their income sources while supporting sustainable practices.

6.3 Case Study 3: The Waitangi Tribunal and New Zealand Businesses – Land Rights and Corporate Accountability

Background: In New Zealand, the Waitangi Tribunal was established to address grievances related to the treatment of the Maori people, particularly concerning land rights. Over the years, the tribunal has played a critical role in facilitating dialogue between the New Zealand government, corporations, and Maori communities. One notable example of corporate accountability in this context is the role played by businesses in respecting and compensating for the historical injustices regarding land ownership and usage.

Key Actions:

- **Consultation and Land Rights:** Several businesses in New Zealand, particularly in the agriculture, forestry, and energy sectors, have worked with the Waitangi Tribunal and Maori communities to ensure that their land use does not infringe upon Maori land rights. These businesses have engaged in consultation processes with the Maori to address land grievances and seek agreements for fair compensation and benefits.

- **Cultural and Economic Integration:** These companies have worked alongside Maori communities to integrate cultural and environmental values into business strategies. The partnerships have involved the transfer of knowledge on sustainable land management and the use of Maori land for eco-tourism or conservation.

- **Formal Apologies and Compensation:** In cases where businesses have contributed to the displacement of Maori communities or the degradation of land, formal apologies and compensation have been agreed upon. This can include financial compensation, as well as reparations in the form of business opportunities or land returned to the communities.

Outcomes:

- **Restoration of Land Rights:** The collaboration between businesses and Maori communities has led to a restoration of rights over ancestral lands, fostering reconciliation and healing.

- **Corporate Accountability:** The cases have set a precedent for corporate accountability in relation to Indigenous land rights, encouraging businesses to take responsibility for their past actions and seek proactive solutions for the future.

- **Sustainable Business Practices:** Maori cultural knowledge has informed business practices in land management, promoting sustainability in the sectors involved.

6.4 Case Study 4: Shell and Indigenous Communities in Canada – Environmental Impact and Energy Transition

Background: Shell, a global energy company, has engaged with Indigenous communities in Canada as part of its efforts to transition to cleaner energy sources while addressing concerns related to the environmental impact of its operations. The company has faced significant opposition from some Indigenous communities, particularly those affected by oil sands extraction in Alberta. However, Shell has also pursued partnerships with Indigenous communities that focus on balancing economic benefits with environmental responsibility.

Key Actions:

- **Environmental and Social Impact Assessments:** Shell works with Indigenous communities to conduct comprehensive environmental and social impact assessments before starting major projects. These assessments include evaluating the potential impacts on traditional lands, water resources, and biodiversity.

- **Collaborative Energy Transition Projects:** As part of its transition to renewable energy, Shell has collaborated with Indigenous communities to develop clean energy projects, such as wind farms and solar energy installations. These projects have provided both economic and environmental benefits for the communities involved.

- **Revenue Sharing and Capacity Building:** Shell has entered into revenue-sharing agreements with Indigenous communities to ensure they benefit from energy projects on their land. The company has also invested in capacity-building initiatives to equip community members with the skills necessary to manage these projects effectively.

Outcomes:

- **Environmental Protection:** The collaborative energy projects have contributed to the reduction of greenhouse gas emissions and environmental degradation while respecting the rights of Indigenous communities.

- **Economic Empowerment:** Through revenue-sharing agreements and capacity-building programs, Indigenous communities have gained economic independence and a stake in the renewable energy transition.

- **Improved Corporate Reputation:** By engaging proactively with Indigenous communities and investing in sustainable energy solutions, Shell has improved its corporate reputation and strengthened its social license to operate in Canada.

6.5 Conclusion: Global Insights and Local Application

These international case studies provide valuable insights for businesses in Australia looking to engage with First Nations communities through their ESG strategies. From sustainable land management in New Zealand to the integration of Indigenous knowledge in Canada's energy transition, businesses can learn from these examples and adapt them to the unique circumstances of Indigenous communities in Australia.

As we continue to move forward in addressing global sustainability challenges, businesses in Australia must Prioritise collaboration, respect for cultural heritage, and environmental responsibility in their dealings with First Nations. These case studies serve as proof that when businesses approach their operations with sensitivity and openness to Indigenous knowledge, both social and environmental outcomes improve, leading to a more sustainable future for all.

Chapter 7: Implementing Global Best Practices in Australia: ESG, Biodiversity, and First Nations

In this chapter, we build on the international case studies presented in Chapter 6 and discuss how businesses in Australia can apply these practices within the local context. The integration of environmental, social, and governance (ESG) principles, with a particular focus on biodiversity and Indigenous rights, is not only a global responsibility but one that directly impacts Australia's future sustainability.

Australia is home to some of the world's most unique and diverse ecosystems, as well as a rich Indigenous cultural heritage that has been stewarded by First Nations people for millennia. However, these ecosystems are under increasing pressure from environmental degradation, and Indigenous communities continue to face socio-economic challenges rooted in colonization and exclusion from decision-making processes. Businesses, by aligning their ESG strategies with both environmental stewardship and respect for First Nations knowledge, can play a key role in tackling these issues.

7.1 Recognising the Need for Contextual Sensitivity in Australia's ESG Practices

Before Australian businesses can implement global best practices, it's essential to understand the unique cultural and environmental landscape in which they are operating. The relationship between First Nations communities and the Australian land, waters, and ecosystems is deeply spiritual and interconnected. Australia's traditional custodians have managed these lands for over 60,000 years, and their knowledge systems, particularly in relation to biodiversity, offer essential insights for contemporary sustainability practices.

However, colonial history, land dispossession, and systemic exclusion have had significant impacts on Indigenous communities. This makes it crucial that Australian businesses actively work to repair these relationships by adopting ethical, transparent, and collaborative approaches to ESG.

7.2 Key Principles for Australian Businesses to Integrate ESG and First Nations Values

To successfully implement global best practices, Australian businesses must ground their ESG initiatives in principles that resonate with the realities of the local environment and First Nations communities. Here, we outline key principles for fostering sustainable, respectful, and impactful partnerships with First Nations:

7.2.1 Cultural Respect and Recognition

Australian businesses must Prioritise cultural respect and recognition when engaging with First Nations. This means not only acknowledging the historical and contemporary significance of the land but actively working to integrate Indigenous knowledge systems into environmental and social decision-making.

- **Actionable Practice:** Begin with formal land acknowledgments in company documents, meetings, and communications. These are powerful statements of respect for the traditional owners and can help set the tone for deeper collaboration.

- **Outcome:** These practices pave the way for stronger relationships, demonstrate respect, and facilitate a more culturally inclusive approach to governance and decision-making.

7.2.2 Collaborating on Biodiversity Conservation

First Nations peoples have long held the key to biodiversity conservation through sustainable land and resource management. This includes practices such as controlled burns to manage fire risks, rotational hunting and fishing to preserve species, and maintaining ecological balance across their territories.

- **Actionable Practice:** Establish joint management arrangements for protected areas, national parks, or conservation projects. Collaborate with Indigenous rangers and land managers who are experts in local biodiversity and ecosystem health.

- **Outcome:** These partnerships can enhance biodiversity conservation while supporting the economic and cultural rights of Indigenous communities. Businesses should look to fund or co-manage projects that restore or protect ecosystems vital to both Indigenous and ecological well-being.

7.2.3 Addressing Land Rights and Environmental Stewardship

One of the most important ways to align with First Nations values is by supporting land rights and engaging in responsible stewardship. Many First Nations communities are actively working to protect their ancestral lands, which hold both cultural and environmental significance.

- **Actionable Practice:** Businesses must ensure that land use does not harm sacred sites or traditional lands. In some cases, this may mean withdrawing from land developments that could have irreversible environmental or cultural impacts. Support land restoration and regeneration projects initiated by First Nations.

- **Outcome:** These efforts build trust, demonstrate corporate social responsibility, and promote long-term sustainability. By respecting First Nations rights, businesses avoid potential reputational risks and legal challenges.

7.3 Practical Steps for Businesses to Align with the SDGs and First Nations Goals

Aligning business operations with the United Nations Sustainable Development Goals (SDGs) and respecting First Nations communities requires an intentional approach that integrates global frameworks with local Indigenous perspectives. Below are actionable steps for Australian businesses to align with both:

7.3.1 Align Business Strategies with SDGs Focused on Indigenous Communities

Australia's commitment to the SDGs, particularly those related to sustainable cities, biodiversity, and responsible consumption, aligns well with the goals of First Nations peoples. Businesses can contribute to the SDGs by ensuring that their activities support the local community and environment while addressing Indigenous needs.

- **Actionable Practice:** Create partnerships that directly contribute to SDGs like affordable and clean energy (SDG

7), decent work and economic growth (SDG 8), and life on land (SDG 15). For example, businesses can fund educational programs focused on sustainability or provide resources for First Nations-led clean energy initiatives.

- **Outcome:** This integrated approach supports the SDGs while benefiting both businesses and Indigenous communities. It also encourages long-term sustainable development.

7.3.2 Promote Economic Development Through Inclusive Business Practices

Supporting First Nations economic independence through business partnerships and initiatives is one of the most impactful ways to reduce poverty and promote social inclusion. Businesses can contribute to SDG 1 (No poverty) and SDG 10 (Reduced inequalities) by ensuring that First Nations communities are given fair economic opportunities.

- **Actionable Practice:** Ensure that Indigenous suppliers are integrated into supply chains, and create mentorship programs that empower First Nations entrepreneurs and workers. Develop inclusive hiring policies that Prioritise diversity and actively recruit Indigenous talent at all levels of the business.

- **Outcome:** These efforts directly contribute to empowering Indigenous communities and fostering inclusive growth. Additionally, businesses gain access to diverse perspectives that can enhance innovation.

7.3.3 Incorporate Traditional Knowledge in Sustainability Projects

Traditional ecological knowledge (TEK) plays a crucial role in preserving biodiversity and protecting ecosystems. This knowledge, passed down through generations, offers valuable insights into climate adaptation and conservation strategies.

- **Actionable Practice:** Integrate TEK into environmental management programs, especially for projects related to land restoration, biodiversity conservation, and water management. For example, traditional knowledge on fire management can be used in controlled burns to reduce bushfire risks.

- **Outcome:** Integrating TEK with modern scientific practices creates more sustainable and culturally appropriate solutions. Businesses that embrace this knowledge demonstrate cultural respect and environmental responsibility.

7.4 Overcoming Challenges and Building Trust

While the integration of First Nations values into business operations is essential, it is not without challenges. For one, there may be historical tensions or mistrust between businesses and Indigenous communities due to past exploitation. Therefore, businesses must be transparent, patient, and committed to long-term engagement.

7.4.1 Navigating Legal and Ethical Barriers

Australia's legal framework around land rights and environmental protection continues to evolve. Businesses must ensure they are compliant with regulations surrounding land use and Indigenous rights, such as the Native Title Act and the Environmental Protection and Biodiversity Conservation Act.

- **Actionable Practice:** Businesses must consult legal experts and engage with Indigenous representatives early in the planning stages of projects to ensure full compliance with local laws.

- **Outcome:** By navigating these legal frameworks thoughtfully, businesses can build a positive relationship with Indigenous communities and avoid costly legal battles.

7.5 Conclusion: Paving the Way for a Sustainable Future

The integration of First Nations communities into Australia's ESG strategies is not just a matter of legal compliance, but also one of mutual benefit. Businesses that align with global sustainability goals while respecting and incorporating the rights, knowledge, and priorities of First Nations communities create a stronger, more resilient future for all.

Chapter 8: Government Policy and the Role of Public Institutions in Supporting ESG and First Nations Partnerships

In this chapter, we will explore the significant role that government policy and public institutions play in fostering sustainable business practices that include the engagement of First Nations communities. Policy frameworks at both the state and federal levels are critical in driving and supporting the integration of environmental, social, and governance (ESG) standards, as well as ensuring the protection and promotion of First Nations rights.

Governments have the power to set the tone for business practices through regulations, incentives, and partnerships. For businesses seeking to align with sustainable development goals (SDGs) and enhance their impact on biodiversity and Indigenous rights, understanding and engaging with government policies is key.

8.1 The Role of Government in Shaping ESG Policy

Governments are fundamental in setting the regulations and frameworks that drive business behavior. In Australia, government policies related to ESG practices often focus on sustainability, environmental protection, and social inclusion. At the same time, First Nations communities are increasingly being recognised as central stakeholders in both policy-making and project implementation.

8.1.1 National Policy and the Net-Zero Emissions Goal

Australia's commitment to achieving net-zero emissions by 2050 provides a vital framework for businesses aiming to transition toward sustainable practices. This policy direction requires a collaborative effort between the government, the private sector, and Indigenous communities, who are often the custodians of much of the land that plays a crucial role in carbon sequestration.

- **Actionable Practice:** Governments must provide clear and supportive policy frameworks for businesses transitioning to net-zero emissions. This can include incentives such as tax breaks or grants for businesses that invest in renewable energy, carbon offset projects, and energy-efficient technologies.

- **Outcome:** Public-private collaboration accelerates the transition to net-zero, with businesses playing a pivotal role in delivering solutions while supporting policies that benefit First Nations communities and biodiversity conservation.

8.1.2 Policy Supporting First Nations Land Rights and Sustainability

The government's policies regarding Indigenous land rights and environmental management directly influence how businesses approach collaboration with First Nations. The Native Title Act 1993, for example, provides legal recognition of the rights of Indigenous Australians to their traditional lands. As a result, businesses must engage with Indigenous communities early in the planning process to ensure their rights are respected and protected.

- **Actionable Practice:** Governments can further empower Indigenous communities by promoting policies that require businesses to consult with and seek consent from First Nations before proceeding with development projects, particularly those affecting land, water, and resources.
- **Outcome:** These policies ensure that First Nations are partners in decision-making and that their cultural, social, and environmental rights are upheld in business operations.

8.2 State and Regional Policies for ESG and First Nations Integration

In addition to federal policies, state and regional governments in Australia play an essential role in guiding and shaping local business practices. Each state may have unique regulations or initiatives aimed at supporting sustainability, biodiversity conservation, and the inclusion of Indigenous communities in economic development.

8.2.1 State-Level Environmental Regulations

State governments in Australia have jurisdiction over a wide range of environmental matters, including the protection of natural resources, biodiversity conservation, and the management of protected areas. Policies at the state level can incentivise businesses to adopt sustainable practices that align with both biodiversity goals and Indigenous rights.

- **Actionable Practice:** States can introduce programs that reward businesses for conserving biodiversity and supporting environmental restoration projects. This might include funding opportunities for conservation initiatives that involve First Nations-led land management.

- **Outcome:** These initiatives promote sustainability at the regional level while simultaneously fostering economic opportunities for Indigenous communities who traditionally manage these lands.

8.2.2 Supporting Indigenous-Run Enterprises and Land Stewardship Programs

Many Indigenous communities in Australia are at the forefront of innovative sustainability practices, particularly in land and water management. Regional governments can play a pivotal role in providing the financial, technical, and logistical support that helps First Nations-led enterprises thrive.

- **Actionable Practice:** States can establish programs that provide grants, mentorship, and market access for First Nations businesses in the sustainability sector. Additionally, partnerships with local environmental groups and businesses can be formalized to ensure these communities are active participants in conservation and resource management.

- **Outcome:** These programs not only support economic development in Indigenous communities but also advance environmental stewardship efforts, making First Nations essential partners in the pursuit of the SDGs.

8.3 Policy Innovations to Strengthen Collaboration between Businesses and First Nations

While many businesses are already taking steps toward sustainable practices, the integration of First Nations communities into ESG frameworks remains an area where more can be done. Governments can lead the way by establishing innovative policies that encourage collaboration and long-term partnerships between businesses and Indigenous peoples.

8.3.1 Establishing Indigenous-Led Sustainability Initiatives

One of the most effective ways that government policy can drive sustainable outcomes is by directly supporting Indigenous-led sustainability initiatives. This might include projects focused on biodiversity conservation, climate adaptation, or ecosystem restoration, with the government providing both funding and legal support.

- **Actionable Practice:** Governments could create funding streams or dedicated agencies that support Indigenous-led projects, from regenerative agriculture to sustainable forestry. In this way, businesses can partner with Indigenous leaders who bring both traditional ecological knowledge and modern sustainability expertise to the table.
- **Outcome:** These policies create lasting economic and environmental benefits for both businesses and Indigenous communities while supporting long-term ecological health.

8.3.2 Supporting Indigenous Land Rights in ESG Reporting

To encourage businesses to engage more meaningfully with First Nations, the government can introduce incentives for companies to include Indigenous rights and land stewardship within their ESG reporting frameworks.

- **Actionable Practice:** Require businesses to disclose how they engage with Indigenous communities, particularly in terms of land use, biodiversity conservation, and the impacts of their operations on traditional lands. This could be aligned with the TCFD (Task Force on Climate-related Financial Disclosures) or similar reporting frameworks.
- **Outcome:** Such policies would promote greater transparency in corporate practices while holding businesses accountable for their environmental and social impacts on First Nations communities.

8.4 Enhancing Corporate Governance through Government-Led ESG Regulations

Strong governance structures are essential to achieving meaningful ESG outcomes. Governments can facilitate this by introducing clear regulations that encourage businesses to consider both environmental and social factors in their decision-making, particularly in relation to Indigenous communities.

8.4.1 Introducing ESG Mandates for Businesses

One of the ways that governments can promote ESG adoption is by requiring businesses to implement ESG practices and report on them transparently. For example, businesses could be legally required to engage with Indigenous stakeholders and demonstrate how their operations contribute to social and environmental goals, including biodiversity protection and community empowerment.

- **Actionable Practice:** Establish regulations that require businesses to disclose their ESG strategies in line with international standards like the GRI (Global Reporting Initiative) or TCFD, with an emphasis on Indigenous rights and biodiversity.

- **Outcome:** This approach would standardise ESG practices, making businesses more accountable and ensuring that they are not just paying lip service to sustainability but actively integrating these values into their core operations.

8.5 Conclusion: Building a Collaborative Future

The alignment of business practices with both the global ESG agenda and the rights of First Nations communities requires a multi-layered approach that integrates governmental policy, corporate responsibility, and community participation. Governments are pivotal in setting the frameworks that encourage collaboration between businesses and Indigenous communities, particularly in the areas of land management, biodiversity conservation, and sustainability.

Chapter 9: Engaging First Nations Communities in ESG Initiatives

In this chapter, we will focus on the critical importance of engaging First Nations communities in environmental, social, and governance (ESG) initiatives. As businesses increasingly align themselves with sustainability goals and biodiversity protection, engaging with the traditional custodians of the land — First Nations peoples — is essential. This collaboration not only respects Indigenous sovereignty but also enriches business practices with traditional ecological knowledge, offering unique solutions to modern sustainability challenges.

A strong, ongoing partnership between businesses and First Nations communities ensures that ESG goals are grounded in cultural context and respect for the land, its biodiversity, and the rights of Indigenous peoples. Engaging with First Nations communities is not merely about seeking permission for development; it is about co-creating sustainable futures that benefit both businesses and the communities they impact.

9.1 Establishing Meaningful Engagement with First Nations Communities

9.1.1 Building Trust Through Consultation and Collaboration

At the heart of any successful relationship with First Nations communities is trust. Businesses need to invest time and resources to understand the unique perspectives, knowledge systems, and priorities of Indigenous communities. Effective engagement begins with consultation and continues with collaboration, ensuring that First Nations are included in decision-making processes that affect their lands and resources.

- **Actionable Practice:** Create consultation frameworks that facilitate open dialogue, respect Indigenous decision-making processes, and provide space for First Nations to share their knowledge and concerns.

- **Outcome:** Trust and mutual respect are established, which paves the way for long-term, sustainable partnerships. Businesses gain invaluable insights from First Nations communities that can enhance their sustainability efforts.

9.1.2 Co-Designing Projects with Indigenous Knowledge

Indigenous communities have centuries of knowledge about local ecosystems, species, and sustainable land management practices. Businesses can benefit greatly from integrating this traditional knowledge with contemporary scientific research. Co-designing projects that involve First Nations peoples ensures that sustainability solutions are context-specific, culturally appropriate, and effective.

- **Actionable Practice:** Involve First Nations in the design, implementation, and evaluation phases of sustainability projects, particularly those related to land and biodiversity conservation.
- **Outcome:** Projects are more likely to be successful and sustainable because they respect the ecological balance and cultural importance of the land, enhancing both environmental and social outcomes.

9.2 Policy and Governance: Building Indigenous Participation into Business Practices

9.2.1 Respecting Traditional Knowledge in Business Decision-Making

Incorporating First Nations knowledge into decision-making is essential for businesses that wish to align their operations with sustainable practices. Recognising the value of this knowledge in governance structures, land management, and environmental stewardship is a step toward reconciliation and shared prosperity.

- **Actionable Practice:** Establish policies that recognise traditional knowledge as an essential component of decision-making, particularly in projects that affect the land and natural resources.
- **Outcome:** Traditional ecological knowledge is respected, and Indigenous peoples have a meaningful role in shaping the future of their land and resources, enhancing their autonomy and participation in governance processes.

9.2.2 Supporting Indigenous Governance Systems

Indigenous governance systems have been proven to be effective in managing natural resources, maintaining biodiversity, and fostering community cohesion. For businesses, supporting Indigenous governance means recognising their right to self-determination and encouraging their leadership in managing resources and projects that directly affect them.

- **Actionable Practice:** Foster partnerships with Indigenous governance bodies to support local decision-making and ensure that development projects align with their laws, traditions, and environmental protection measures.
- **Outcome:** Indigenous communities take a lead role in managing their lands and resources, creating a more just and sustainable development process that benefits both communities and businesses.

9.3 Strengthening Economic and Social Development Through ESG

9.3.1 Providing Economic Opportunities for Indigenous Communities

Economic development should be an integral part of any ESG initiative involving First Nations. By providing opportunities for Indigenous businesses, employees, and entrepreneurs, businesses can help uplift these communities, reduce inequality, and create a more inclusive economy.

- **Actionable Practice:** Establish hiring policies that Prioritise Indigenous talent, invest in training programs, and support Indigenous-owned businesses through procurement practices.
- **Outcome:** First Nations communities benefit from economic opportunities that enhance their socio-economic development, reduce poverty, and create jobs within their communities.

9.3.2 Supporting Cultural and Social Well-being

Supporting the cultural well-being of First Nations is as important as the economic and environmental aspects of sustainability. Initiatives should focus not just on land and resources but also on the preservation and revitalization of cultural practices and language, which are essential to the identity and cohesion of First Nations communities.

- **Actionable Practice:** Invest in programs that promote cultural heritage, including language preservation, traditional ecological knowledge sharing, and cultural education.
- **Outcome:** The preservation of First Nations culture and traditions strengthens community ties, supports identity, and fosters a sense of pride and belonging, while contributing to social sustainability.

9.4 Overcoming Challenges: Practical Solutions for Businesses

9.4.1 Addressing Barriers to Indigenous Engagement

One of the challenges businesses face when working with First Nations communities is overcoming the historical and systemic barriers that have often excluded them from decision-making processes. It's crucial for businesses to recognise these barriers and actively work to dismantle them.

- **Actionable Practice:** Commit to cultural competency training for all employees, particularly those working directly with Indigenous communities, to ensure that they understand the historical context and contemporary challenges faced by these communities.
- **Outcome:** Cultural competency fosters a respectful working environment, enabling businesses to engage meaningfully with Indigenous peoples and avoid inadvertently perpetuating inequalities.

9.4.2 Building Long-Term Relationships

Sustainability efforts are most effective when they are built on long-term relationships, rather than one-off projects. Businesses must Prioritise long-term, enduring partnerships with First Nations, ensuring that engagement is not just for the duration of a project but ongoing.

- **Actionable Practice:** Create long-term partnership agreements with First Nations that include clear, mutually agreed goals and measures of success. These partnerships should be flexible enough to evolve as community needs and business operations change over time.

- **Outcome:** Long-term relationships lead to sustained impact, stronger trust, and the ability to adapt to changing circumstances, all while promoting environmental, social, and economic sustainability.

9.5 Conclusion: The Path Toward True Collaboration

For businesses to truly align with the principles of ESG, they must not only commit to protecting biodiversity and fostering sustainability but also to ensuring that First Nations communities are actively involved in and benefit from these efforts. This collaborative approach is not just a moral imperative but also a strategic advantage. By engaging First Nations in meaningful, culturally respectful, and mutually beneficial ways, businesses can unlock new opportunities for innovation, sustainability, and long-term growth.

Chapter 10: Implementing Accountability and Transparency in ESG Initiatives with First Nations

In this chapter, we will delve into how businesses can ensure that their engagement with First Nations communities and biodiversity efforts are transparent, accountable, and impactful. Accountability and transparency are essential elements in any effective ESG initiative. When working with First Nations communities, it is particularly crucial to foster trust and demonstrate that promises are being upheld through measurable actions. This chapter will outline frameworks and best practices that businesses can use to track, report, and continuously improve their sustainability efforts while ensuring that their work with First Nations communities is done respectfully, ethically, and sustainably.

10.1 Establishing Accountability Frameworks for Indigenous Engagement

10.1.1 Defining Clear Roles and Responsibilities

When engaging First Nations communities, businesses must define clear roles and responsibilities for all stakeholders involved. This not only ensures effective collaboration but also ensures that First Nations communities have a central role in decision-making and governance processes. Clear roles can be defined through memorandums of understanding (MOUs), partnership agreements, and joint governance frameworks, allowing each party to be accountable for their contributions.

- **Actionable Practice:** Develop partnership agreements with First Nations communities that clearly outline roles, responsibilities, and expectations for both businesses and Indigenous stakeholders.

- **Outcome:** Clear accountability fosters mutual respect, ensuring that both parties contribute equally and transparently to achieving the shared sustainability goals.

10.1.2 Implementing Independent Oversight

Independent oversight is a critical component of accountability. Third-party audits or reviews can help evaluate the effectiveness of ESG initiatives, ensuring that they are aligned with both business goals and the priorities of First Nations communities. This oversight can provide additional assurance to all stakeholders that projects are being implemented ethically and that environmental and social outcomes are being met.

- **Actionable Practice:** Engage independent auditors or external evaluators to assess the impact of ESG initiatives and the collaboration with First Nations communities.

- **Outcome:** Third-party verification enhances transparency, ensuring that all practices and impacts are fully assessed, making the initiative credible and building trust with both communities and stakeholders.

10.2 Reporting and Monitoring ESG Efforts

10.2.1 Regular Monitoring of Environmental and Social Impacts

To ensure accountability, businesses need to implement regular monitoring systems that track the environmental and social impacts of their operations, especially those affecting First Nations communities and biodiversity. By monitoring these impacts, businesses can identify areas of improvement and respond to challenges proactively.

- **Actionable Practice:** Implement tracking systems to monitor key performance indicators (KPIs) related to biodiversity conservation, emissions reductions, and community engagement efforts. For instance, businesses can use digital platforms or software to track metrics on land and water health, carbon footprints, and progress on biodiversity projects.

- **Outcome:** Ongoing monitoring helps identify problems early, allowing businesses to take corrective actions in real time and ensure they remain on track with their ESG goals.

10.2.2 Transparent Reporting to Stakeholders

Transparency is at the heart of effective ESG reporting. For businesses to demonstrate their commitment to First Nations sustainability and biodiversity, they must consistently report on their progress, challenges, and outcomes. Public reporting provides all stakeholders — from investors and customers to the First Nations communities — with access to accurate, up-to-date information about the business's ESG performance. Reports should adhere to established frameworks such as the Global Reporting Initiative (GRI), TCFD, or the United Nations Global Compact.

- **Actionable Practice:** Commit to providing annual or bi-annual sustainability reports that detail both successes and areas for improvement in terms of biodiversity conservation, First Nations engagement, and the achievement of SDGs.
- **Outcome:** Transparent, comprehensive reports build stakeholder confidence, demonstrating a business's dedication to sustainability and ethical practices. This also helps ensure that all efforts are aligned with broader sustainability and community development goals.

10.3 Continuous Improvement and Adaptation

10.3.1 Integrating Feedback Loops from First Nations Communities

Feedback from First Nations communities is crucial for ensuring that ESG initiatives are not only successful but also respectful and culturally appropriate. Businesses must establish formal channels through which community feedback can be collected, analysed, and integrated into decision-making processes. These channels can include community meetings, surveys, and workshops, as well as advisory boards or councils that allow community members to engage directly with business leaders.

- **Actionable Practice:** Create formal feedback mechanisms that enable First Nations communities to provide input on the effectiveness of sustainability initiatives, and ensure that this feedback is incorporated into ongoing project designs and future strategies.
- **Outcome:** Continuous feedback loops help businesses refine their practices and adapt strategies based on the needs and concerns of First Nations communities, ensuring that ESG initiatives remain relevant and effective.

10.3.2 Adaptability to Changing Circumstances

The world of ESG is dynamic, and so is the landscape in which First Nations communities operate. Climate change, evolving policies, and social changes may all necessitate shifts in business strategies. A commitment to continuous improvement means that businesses should regularly review and adapt their approaches to sustainability to reflect new information, changing priorities, and emerging challenges.

- **Actionable Practice:** Regularly review and revise ESG strategies to stay aligned with the latest scientific findings, technological innovations, and feedback from First Nations communities.

- **Outcome:** Adaptable strategies ensure that businesses remain resilient in the face of environmental, economic, or social changes, and continue to contribute positively to First Nations sustainability goals.

10.4 The Role of Technology and Innovation in ESG Accountability

10.4.1 Leveraging Technology for Better ESG Tracking and Reporting

Technology plays an increasingly important role in driving ESG accountability. From digital tracking systems that monitor carbon emissions to mobile apps that enable real-time reporting of biodiversity health, technology can help businesses track their progress with greater precision and transparency. Moreover, technologies such as blockchain can ensure the security and integrity of ESG data, providing stakeholders with the confidence that reports are accurate and tamper-proof.

- **Actionable Practice:** Invest in innovative technologies such as blockchain for transparency in reporting and AI-powered tools for real-time monitoring of environmental impacts.

- **Outcome:** Improved tracking and reporting capabilities ensure that ESG initiatives are accurately measured, reported, and verified, enhancing the business's credibility and trustworthiness.

10.5 Conclusion: The Path Forward for Accountability in ESG Initiatives

As businesses continue to embrace ESG principles, accountability and transparency will be paramount to achieving long-term success, particularly in their engagement with First Nations communities and biodiversity protection. By implementing clear governance frameworks, monitoring performance, providing transparent reporting, and adapting strategies based on feedback and new information, businesses can ensure that they are making meaningful, sustainable progress.

This chapter has outlined a roadmap for businesses to implement the necessary structures and practices for accountability and transparency in ESG efforts.

Chapter 11: Building a Culture of Sustainability Within the Organization

In this chapter, we will focus on how businesses can foster a culture of sustainability, ensuring that their commitment to environmental stewardship, First Nations engagement, and biodiversity preservation is ingrained at every level of the organization. The goal is to make sustainability a core part of business operations, where every employee, from leadership to the front lines, feels responsible for contributing to sustainability goals. A strong sustainability culture not only drives environmental and social change but also promotes a sense of collective responsibility and purpose, making sustainability a shared value.

11.1 Leadership Commitment to Sustainability

11.1.1 Establishing Sustainability as a Core Business Value

For sustainability to become a core value, leadership must not only endorse but actively champion sustainable practices. When leaders demonstrate a commitment to sustainability, it sends a clear message throughout the organization that these efforts are a priority. Leadership should integrate sustainability into the company's mission, vision, and core values, and should consistently model sustainable practices.

- **Actionable Practice:** Ensure that sustainability is part of the organisation's overall strategic objectives, integrated into key business decisions, and reflected in leadership communication.

- **Outcome:** When leaders consistently Prioritise sustainability, it sets a tone from the top that encourages employees at all levels to adopt and support these values.

11.1.2 Leading by Example: Sustainable Practices at the Top

Leadership should lead by example, incorporating sustainable practices into their day-to-day activities. This could include everything from making environmentally conscious decisions in office operations to supporting sustainable supply chains and First Nations-led initiatives. By demonstrating commitment to sustainability through action, leaders inspire employees to follow suit.

- **Actionable Practice:** Leadership should model sustainable behaviors such as reducing energy consumption, adopting electric vehicles, and supporting green energy initiatives.

- **Outcome:** When leadership practices what they preach, employees are more likely to embrace sustainability within their own work practices.

11.2 Employee Engagement in Sustainability Initiatives

11.2.1 Empowering Employees to Drive Sustainability

Employees are the foundation of any successful sustainability initiative. For sustainability to thrive, every employee must feel empowered to contribute to the organisation's goals. This can be achieved by engaging employees in the design, execution, and tracking of sustainability initiatives. Providing employees with the tools, knowledge, and autonomy to make sustainability a part of their role can have a powerful impact on the organisation's overall performance.

- **Actionable Practice:** Develop sustainability teams or committees that encourage employees to contribute ideas, track progress, and lead initiatives within their departments or teams.

- **Outcome:** Empowered employees will feel more invested in the organisation's sustainability goals and contribute their creativity and innovation to solving environmental and social challenges.

11.2.2 Employee Sustainability Training and Development

Education is key to creating a sustainability-driven culture. By offering training programs, workshops, and resources on sustainability practices, businesses can equip employees with the knowledge and skills needed to contribute effectively to sustainability efforts. These programs can range from basic environmental awareness to more advanced training in specific areas such as carbon accounting, biodiversity monitoring, and sustainable sourcing practices.

- **Actionable Practice:** Implement a comprehensive sustainability training program that educates employees on climate change, biodiversity, and social justice issues, as well as how to apply this knowledge to their daily tasks.

- **Outcome:** Well-informed employees are better equipped to make decisions that align with the company's sustainability objectives, driving continuous improvement.

11.3 Fostering Collaboration and Engagement Across Departments

11.3.1 Encouraging Cross-Departmental Collaboration

One of the keys to successful sustainability initiatives is collaboration across all departments. Sustainability is not the responsibility of one team; it should be embedded into all aspects of business operations, from finance and marketing to operations and human resources. By fostering collaboration and sharing insights across departments, organisations can develop holistic solutions that address sustainability from multiple angles.

- **Actionable Practice:** Create cross-departmental teams focused on key sustainability goals, such as reducing waste, improving energy efficiency, or supporting First Nations-led biodiversity projects.

- **Outcome:** Collaborative efforts ensure that sustainability is integrated into all areas of business, resulting in more effective, wide-reaching solutions.

11.3.2 Building Internal Networks and Communities of Practice

Communities of practice, both formal and informal, can help sustain momentum around sustainability efforts within an organization. These networks allow employees from different departments to share ideas, best practices, and lessons learned, ultimately contributing to the overall sustainability objectives of the business.

- **Actionable Practice:** Establish internal networks for sustainability advocates to collaborate and share insights and best practices. Encourage informal groups and clubs focused on sustainability.

- **Outcome:** Networks foster knowledge-sharing, create a sense of community around sustainability, and generate new ideas that can drive further improvements.

11.4 Engaging with First Nations Communities and Other External Stakeholders

11.4.1 Collaborative Partnerships for Sustainable Development

Collaboration with First Nations communities and other external stakeholders is essential for effective sustainability initiatives. Building strong, mutually beneficial partnerships allows businesses to tap into local knowledge, strengthen community ties, and contribute meaningfully to social and environmental sustainability. These partnerships should be based on mutual respect, shared goals, and a long-term commitment to improving environmental and social outcomes.

- **Actionable Practice:** Actively engage with First Nations communities in the design and implementation of sustainability projects, ensuring that their knowledge and priorities are integral to the business's strategy.

- **Outcome:** Collaboration with First Nations communities and stakeholders ensures that sustainability initiatives are more relevant, culturally appropriate, and impactful.

11.4.2 Listening and Responding to Stakeholder Feedback

Engagement doesn't stop once a partnership is established. Ongoing communication with stakeholders, including First Nations communities, environmental organisations, and customers, is crucial to maintaining trust and ensuring that initiatives are meeting their goals. Regular feedback loops allow businesses to adapt their strategies based on input from those directly affected by their operations.

- **Actionable Practice:** Develop formal feedback mechanisms to gather insights from stakeholders on sustainability projects, and ensure that this feedback is actively incorporated into future actions.

- **Outcome:** Listening to and responding to feedback strengthens relationships with stakeholders and enhances the effectiveness of sustainability efforts.

11.5 Measuring and Celebrating Progress

11.5.1 Tracking and Celebrating Sustainability Milestones

Measuring progress is essential for demonstrating the effectiveness of sustainability initiatives and keeping momentum high within the organization. Establishing clear, measurable goals for sustainability allows businesses to track progress over time and make necessary adjustments. Celebrating milestones along the way helps maintain enthusiasm and commitment to the long-term sustainability journey.

- **Actionable Practice:** Set specific sustainability targets (e.g., reducing carbon emissions, conserving water, increasing renewable energy use) and celebrate achievements in meetings, internal communications, and sustainability reports.

- **Outcome:** Celebrating success builds morale and motivates employees to continue their efforts while showcasing the company's commitment to sustainability to external stakeholders.

11.5.2 Aligning Employee Performance with Sustainability Goals

Aligning employee performance metrics with sustainability objectives helps ensure that everyone in the organization is working towards the same goals. By making sustainability an integral part of performance evaluations, businesses can ensure that all employees are responsible for contributing to the organisation's sustainability initiatives.

- **Actionable Practice:** Incorporate sustainability targets into employee performance reviews and offer incentives for achieving key sustainability milestones.

- **Outcome:** Aligning individual goals with the business's sustainability goals helps to create a culture of collective responsibility and ensures that all employees contribute to the organisation's ESG objectives.

11.6 Conclusion: Sustainability as a Core Business Value

Building a culture of sustainability requires time, effort, and commitment from every level of the organization. As businesses work to engage employees, collaborate with First Nations communities, and lead by example, they must remain adaptable and transparent in their approach. From leadership to operational teams, every employee plays a role in ensuring the success of sustainability initiatives.

Chapter 12: Innovation and Technology Driving Sustainability

In the previous chapter, we explored how businesses can build a culture of sustainability, empowering their employees and engaging with external stakeholders. Now, we shift focus to the tools and technologies that can accelerate the transition to a sustainable future. Innovation and technology play pivotal roles in scaling sustainability efforts, reducing environmental footprints, and creating value in alignment with the United Nations Sustainable Development Goals (SDGs).

This chapter will examine the role of emerging technologies, digital transformation, and innovation in driving corporate sustainability, with an emphasis on the potential for improving energy efficiency, reducing carbon emissions, and enhancing the resilience of ecosystems. By leveraging cutting-edge technologies, businesses can create scalable, impactful sustainability solutions that also generate economic value.

12.1 The Role of Technology in Climate Action

12.1.1 Renewable Energy Technologies

One of the most significant ways businesses can contribute to the global transition to net-zero emissions is by investing in renewable energy sources. Solar, wind, and geothermal energy have emerged as leading solutions to reduce reliance on fossil fuels, and new technological advancements are continuously improving their efficiency and cost-effectiveness.

- **Actionable Practice:** Invest in renewable energy technologies like solar panels, wind turbines, or geothermal systems, either on-site or through power purchase agreements (PPAs).
- **Outcome:** Reduces greenhouse gas emissions and supports the transition to a clean energy future.

12.1.2 Energy Storage Solutions

As renewable energy sources like solar and wind generate power intermittently, energy storage solutions are crucial for ensuring a reliable energy supply. Advanced battery technologies, such as lithium-ion and solid-state batteries, provide businesses with the ability to store energy for use during periods of high demand or when renewable sources are not generating enough power.

- **Actionable Practice:** Invest in energy storage systems to ensure that excess renewable energy can be stored and used when demand peaks.
- **Outcome:** Ensures energy resilience, reduces reliance on the grid, and promotes the use of renewable energy even during low-generation periods.

12.1.3 Smart Energy Management Systems

Smart energy management systems use real-time data to monitor and optimise energy consumption across an organisation's facilities. These systems, powered by the Internet of Things (IoT), can detect inefficiencies, automatically adjust energy usage, and provide actionable insights for continuous improvement.

- **Actionable Practice:** Implement smart meters and energy management systems to monitor energy use, identify inefficiencies, and make data-driven decisions to reduce consumption.
- **Outcome:** Lowers operational energy costs, reduces emissions, and increases the overall efficiency of business operations.

12.2 Harnessing Big Data and Artificial Intelligence (AI)

12.2.1 Big Data in Sustainability Monitoring

Big data plays a vital role in environmental monitoring, enabling businesses to track, analyse, and predict environmental trends. By harnessing large datasets, companies can measure their environmental impact, understand sustainability performance, and identify areas for improvement.

- **Actionable Practice:** Use big data analytics to collect and analyse environmental data from various sources, including energy consumption, water use, emissions, and waste generation.
- **Outcome:** Provides a comprehensive understanding of the company's environmental footprint and helps inform decision-making and policy development.

12.2.2 AI and Machine Learning for Efficiency Optimization

Artificial Intelligence (AI) and machine learning algorithms can optimise business operations by analysing large volumes of data to find patterns, improve processes, and suggest efficiencies. These technologies can be used to streamline supply chains, reduce waste, and optimise production processes.

- **Actionable Practice:** Integrate AI-driven solutions into operational workflows to optimise processes like supply chain logistics, inventory management, and energy usage.

- **Outcome:** Increases operational efficiency, reduces waste, and supports sustainable resource management.

12.3 Sustainable Supply Chains and Blockchain Technology

12.3.1 Blockchain for Transparency in Supply Chains

Blockchain technology can play a key role in ensuring transparency and sustainability in supply chains. By providing a secure and immutable record of transactions, blockchain allows businesses and consumers to trace the entire lifecycle of a product—from raw materials to end-of-life disposal—ensuring that each step aligns with sustainability principles.

- **Actionable Practice:** Implement blockchain to track and verify the sustainability of raw materials, ethical labor practices, and carbon emissions across the supply chain.

- **Outcome:** Ensures transparency and accountability, improves traceability, and fosters trust in the company's sustainability practices.

12.3.2 Circular Economy and Product Lifecycle Management

The circular economy is based on the principles of designing products for reuse, recycling, and regeneration. Digital technologies, such as IoT and blockchain, can facilitate circular business models by tracking the use, disposal, and recycling of products. This contributes to reducing waste and maximizing resource efficiency.

- **Actionable Practice:** Implement IoT-enabled product tracking systems to monitor product usage and end-of-life disposal, supporting the transition to a circular economy.

- **Outcome:** Reduces waste, extends the lifespan of materials, and fosters a more sustainable use of resources.

12.4 Green Finance and Sustainable Investment

12.4.1 Sustainable Investment Tools

Green finance refers to investments that support environmental sustainability projects, such as renewable energy, energy efficiency, and climate adaptation efforts. Financial institutions and businesses are increasingly using sustainable investment tools like green bonds, ESG (Environmental, Social, and Governance) funds, and sustainability-linked loans to fund projects that promote climate action.

- **Actionable Practice:** Offer or invest in green bonds and other sustainable financial products to fund environmental initiatives, such as renewable energy projects or carbon reduction efforts.

- **Outcome:** Increases access to capital for sustainability projects and helps shift financial flows toward environmentally responsible investments.

12.4.2 Integration of ESG Factors in Investment Decisions

Businesses can integrate ESG factors into their investment strategies to Prioritise environmental and social considerations. By incorporating ESG factors into financial models, organisations can align their portfolios with climate goals and promote long-term sustainable growth.

- **Actionable Practice:** Adopt ESG criteria when making investment decisions, ensuring that projects meet sustainability, social impact, and governance standards.

- **Outcome:** Creates long-term value by mitigating environmental risks, attracting sustainable investors, and contributing to global sustainability goals.

12.5 The Future of Sustainability: Embracing Innovation

12.5.1 The Role of Emerging Technologies

Emerging technologies such as quantum computing, nanotechnology, and advanced materials are poised to revolutionize sustainability efforts. These technologies can provide innovative solutions to environmental challenges, from clean energy generation to waste management and resource conservation.

- **Actionable Practice:** Keep abreast of emerging technologies that have the potential to enhance sustainability, and explore ways to integrate these technologies into business strategies.
- **Outcome:** Future-proofs the business by leveraging cutting-edge solutions to meet environmental and sustainability targets.

12.5.2 The Importance of Adaptive Innovation

As environmental challenges evolve, businesses must remain flexible and adaptive in their approach to innovation. Companies that invest in research and development (R&D) to find new ways of reducing emissions, conserving resources, and improving sustainability will be best positioned to lead in the green economy.

- **Actionable Practice:** Foster a culture of innovation by investing in R&D, and partner with academic institutions or startups focused on sustainability solutions.
- **Outcome:** Ensures continuous improvement and innovation, positioning the organization as a leader in sustainability.

12.6 Conclusion: Leveraging Innovation for a Sustainable Future

Innovation and technology offer immense potential for businesses to drive sustainability and mitigate environmental impacts. By adopting renewable energy, improving energy efficiency, harnessing the power of AI and blockchain, and investing in green finance, businesses can significantly contribute to climate action. However, it is important to note that these innovations must be applied thoughtfully and integrated into broader sustainability strategies to be truly effective.

Chapter 13: Monitoring, Measuring, and Reporting Sustainability Progress

In the previous chapter, we discussed the critical role of innovation and technology in accelerating sustainable practices. Now, as we move toward implementing these strategies, the next challenge is how to effectively track progress, measure performance, and report on sustainability initiatives. Businesses must not only focus on achieving sustainability goals but also on transparently sharing those results with stakeholders. This ensures that companies are held accountable, enables continual improvement, and demonstrates commitment to environmental, social, and governance (ESG) principles.

This chapter delves into the importance of monitoring, measuring, and reporting sustainability efforts in a way that is both transparent and impactful. We will explore the tools, metrics, and frameworks available for assessing progress, as well as strategies for communicating results to stakeholders.

13.1 The Importance of Monitoring and Measuring Sustainability Performance

13.1.1 Why Measurement is Essential for Sustainability

Effective monitoring and measurement are at the heart of any successful sustainability strategy. Without clear and reliable data, businesses cannot accurately assess their environmental impact, track progress toward sustainability goals, or identify areas for improvement. Furthermore, consistent measurement ensures that organisations stay on track and can make data-driven decisions for long-term sustainability.

- **Actionable Practice:** Regularly assess the environmental, social, and economic impact of business operations using a combination of quantitative and qualitative metrics.
- **Outcome:** Provides actionable insights into sustainability performance and highlights areas for improvement or scaling efforts.

13.1.2 Key Performance Indicators (KPIs) for Sustainability

Key Performance Indicators (KPIs) are essential for measuring progress toward sustainability goals. These indicators allow businesses to quantify their environmental and social impacts, evaluate their efforts, and track their alignment with global frameworks like the United Nations SDGs.

- **Actionable Practice:** Develop KPIs tailored to your organisation's sustainability goals, such as greenhouse gas (GHG) emissions reduction, energy efficiency improvements, water conservation, waste reduction, and community engagement.
- **Outcome:** Allows businesses to track performance over time, compare results with targets, and make informed decisions on where to improve or adjust strategies.

13.2 Tools and Frameworks for Reporting Sustainability Performance

13.2.1 Global Reporting Initiative (GRI) Standards

The Global Reporting Initiative (GRI) is one of the most widely adopted frameworks for sustainability reporting. It provides businesses with a structured approach to report on various ESG metrics, covering economic, environmental, and social impacts. GRI allows for consistency and comparability in reporting, making it easier for organisations to communicate their sustainability efforts to stakeholders.

- **Actionable Practice:** Adopt the GRI Standards to create detailed sustainability reports that align with international best practices.
- **Outcome:** Improves transparency, fosters stakeholder trust, and aligns the organisation's reporting with globally recognised standards.

13.2.2 Task Force on Climate-related Financial Disclosures (TCFD)

The TCFD framework focuses specifically on climate-related risks and opportunities, guiding companies in disclosing how climate change impacts their governance, strategy, and financial performance. TCFD recommendations are especially relevant for businesses seeking to mitigate the financial risks of climate change while demonstrating their commitment to climate action.

- **Actionable Practice:** Implement TCFD recommendations by reporting on climate-related governance, strategy, risk management, and metrics.
- **Outcome:** Aligns reporting with climate resilience efforts, provides investors and stakeholders with clear climate-related information, and improves long-term strategic planning.

13.2.3 Sustainability Accounting Standards Board (SASB)

The SASB standards offer an industry-specific approach to sustainability reporting, focusing on material ESG factors that are likely to impact financial performance. These standards help companies disclose sustainability performance data in a way that meets the needs of investors, providing a clear picture of the risks and opportunities that could affect business value.

- **Actionable Practice:** Use SASB standards to report on ESG factors that are material to your industry, focusing on aspects that affect both financial performance and long-term sustainability.
- **Outcome:** Provides investors with relevant, comparable ESG data, enhancing the organisation's credibility and transparency.

13.2.4 Integrated Reporting Framework

Integrated reporting is a holistic approach that combines financial and non-financial performance into one report. This framework emphasizes the value of all capitals—financial, manufactured, intellectual, human, social, and natural—demonstrating how an organisation's activities contribute to the creation of long-term value.

- **Actionable Practice:** Adopt an integrated reporting approach that links sustainability and financial performance, showcasing how ESG efforts drive long-term value creation.
- **Outcome:** Provides a comprehensive view of the organisation's sustainability journey, connecting performance with broader business goals and strategy.

13.3 Best Practices for Transparent and Impactful Reporting

13.3.1 Stakeholder Engagement in Reporting

Transparency is essential for sustainability reporting. Engaging stakeholders—ranging from investors and employees to communities and suppliers—ensures that the information shared is relevant, credible, and aligned with stakeholder expectations. Businesses must engage these stakeholders not only in the reporting process but also in decision-making and strategy development.

- **Actionable Practice:** Regularly engage stakeholders through consultations, surveys, and feedback sessions to ensure reporting is comprehensive and reflective of their concerns.
- **Outcome:** Ensures that sustainability reports are responsive to stakeholder needs and enhances the organisation's credibility.

13.3.2 Use of Technology for Real-Time Reporting

Advancements in technology have enabled businesses to move beyond annual sustainability reports. Real-time reporting systems, powered by IoT and data analytics, allow organisations to track sustainability performance on an ongoing basis, providing immediate insights into key metrics.

- **Actionable Practice:** Implement real-time sustainability tracking systems that monitor energy use, waste management, water consumption, and emissions.
- **Outcome:** Improves decision-making by providing up-to-date data, making it easier to identify inefficiencies or risks early and adjust strategies accordingly.

13.3.3 Emphasize Storytelling and Impact

While quantitative data is important, storytelling can also play a powerful role in sustainability reporting. Sharing success stories, lessons learned, and the broader impact of sustainability initiatives humanizes the data and helps stakeholders connect with the organisation's efforts.

- **Actionable Practice:** Include qualitative stories in sustainability reports to highlight the tangible benefits of initiatives on communities, ecosystems, and the business.
- **Outcome:** Increases emotional engagement with stakeholders, fostering stronger support for sustainability programs and initiatives.

13.4 The Future of Reporting and Measuring Sustainability

13.4.1 Advancements in ESG Reporting Tools

The field of ESG reporting is rapidly evolving. Emerging technologies such as artificial intelligence (AI), machine learning (ML), and blockchain are set to transform the way companies report and manage sustainability data. AI can analyse vast amounts of data to uncover hidden trends, while blockchain offers transparent, tamper-proof reporting solutions that provide real-time updates on ESG metrics.

- **Actionable Practice:** Stay ahead of emerging trends in reporting by adopting new technologies that enhance data accuracy, transparency, and real-time monitoring.
- **Outcome:** Enables better-informed decision-making and strengthens the credibility of sustainability reports.

13.4.2 Aligning with Global Reporting Initiatives

As global awareness of sustainability challenges grows, more frameworks, standards, and regulations will emerge. Organisations must stay aligned with evolving guidelines, ensuring their reports are not only transparent but also forward-looking and in line with international sustainability frameworks.

- **Actionable Practice:** Continuously update sustainability reporting practices to stay aligned with emerging global standards like the Global Reporting Initiative (GRI), the UN Global Compact, and others.
- **Outcome:** Ensures that reporting practices remain relevant, globally accepted, and robust enough to address future challenges.

13.5 Conclusion: The Power of Transparency and Accountability

Monitoring, measuring, and reporting sustainability progress is not just a regulatory requirement—it's a core component of a business's long-term success. Transparent and accountable reporting allows businesses to demonstrate their commitment to sustainability, engage stakeholders, and drive continuous improvement. By leveraging advanced reporting frameworks, technologies, and stakeholder engagement, businesses can elevate their sustainability performance and foster greater trust and collaboration across industries.

Chapter 14: Building Resilient and Adaptive Sustainability Strategies

As businesses continue to navigate the evolving landscape of sustainability, it is essential to understand that resilience is no longer a luxury but a necessity. In Chapter 13, we explored the tools and frameworks for measuring and reporting sustainability progress. Now, we turn our focus to developing strategies that allow businesses to remain adaptable and resilient in the face of increasing climate, social, and economic pressures.

This chapter will explore how organisations can build sustainability strategies that are not only effective but also robust and adaptable, ensuring that they can weather unexpected challenges, stay ahead of market shifts, and remain aligned with global sustainability objectives.

14.1 The Concept of Resilience in Sustainability

14.1.1 What is Resilience in the Context of Sustainability?

Resilience in sustainability refers to the capacity of a business to anticipate, prepare for, respond to, and recover from disruptions while continuing to deliver long-term environmental, social, and economic value. In the face of climate change, resource scarcity, social inequality, and economic volatility, organisations must have the ability to adapt their operations, supply chains, and business models.

- **Actionable Practice:** Assess the potential risks to your business from climate change, resource depletion, and social unrest. Build resilience by diversifying operations and creating adaptable business models.
- **Outcome:** Ensures the long-term viability of the business while minimizing the impact of disruptions.

14.1.2 Why Resilience is Critical to Sustainability

With the increasing frequency of extreme weather events, evolving regulations, and shifts in consumer behavior, the ability to adapt quickly and efficiently to change is essential. Businesses that integrate resilience into their sustainability strategies can capitalize on emerging opportunities while minimizing exposure to risks.

- **Actionable Practice:** Use scenario planning and stress-testing to identify potential vulnerabilities in your supply chain, workforce, and operational processes.
- **Outcome:** Provides insights into where your business is most vulnerable and enables you to take proactive steps to mitigate risks.

14.2 Integrating Flexibility and Adaptability into Sustainability Strategies

14.2.1 Developing Adaptive Strategies for Changing Conditions

An adaptable sustainability strategy is one that allows a business to pivot quickly in response to changing circumstances. As climate-related risks, regulatory changes, and market expectations evolve, businesses need to adjust their sustainability plans to remain competitive.

One way to build adaptability is by adopting a **dynamic approach** to resource management, energy efficiency, and waste reduction. Companies must be prepared to recalibrate their goals and tactics as new technologies emerge, customer demands shift, or external conditions change.

- **Actionable Practice:** Establish a continuous feedback loop where sustainability strategies are regularly reviewed and adjusted based on changing conditions or new information.
- **Outcome:** Ensures the organization stays nimble and can adjust to both incremental changes and sudden disruptions.

14.2.2 Building Diverse, Resilient Supply Chains

A resilient supply chain is one that can absorb shocks, whether they are caused by extreme weather, political instability, or economic downturns. Diversifying supply sources, incorporating local suppliers, and leveraging digital tools to track supply chain performance are key strategies for enhancing resilience.

- **Actionable Practice:** Map your supply chain to identify risks and diversify suppliers across geographic regions and industries. Invest in digital tools and platforms that provide real-time visibility and predictive analytics for better decision-making.

- **Outcome:** Reduces dependency on a single source and enhances the overall resilience of your operations.

14.3 The Role of Stakeholders in Building Resilience

14.3.1 Engaging Stakeholders in Sustainability and Resilience Efforts

Stakeholder engagement is a key component of building resilience. It allows businesses to identify emerging risks, build trust, and collaborate on sustainability initiatives. By engaging with a broad range of stakeholders—employees, suppliers, customers, communities, and governments—businesses can ensure that their sustainability strategies are aligned with the needs and expectations of those who are impacted by their operations.

- **Actionable Practice:** Regularly communicate with stakeholders through surveys, consultations, and partnership programs to understand their concerns and gather feedback on sustainability initiatives.
- **Outcome:** Helps ensure that sustainability efforts are aligned with the values of key stakeholders, increasing buy-in and collaboration.

14.3.2 Collaborating with External Experts and NGOs

Partnerships with external experts and non-governmental organisations (NGOs) can help businesses stay informed about the latest sustainability trends, technologies, and best practices. These collaborations provide valuable insights and help businesses integrate cutting-edge solutions into their resilience strategies.

- **Actionable Practice:** Engage with environmental NGOs, climate scientists, and sustainability consultants to gain insights into emerging risks and opportunities for innovation.
- **Outcome:** Strengthens your organisation's resilience by incorporating external expertise and perspectives into decision-making.

14.4 The Role of Technology in Enhancing Resilience

14.4.1 Leveraging Technology for Adaptive Sustainability Practices

Advancements in technology play a significant role in enhancing the resilience of sustainability strategies. Digital tools, including Artificial Intelligence (AI), machine learning (ML), and big data analytics, can provide real-time insights into operations, help forecast environmental risks, and optimise resource management.

- **Actionable Practice:** Invest in AI-driven platforms that can predict environmental risks, monitor resource consumption, and suggest improvements for energy efficiency.
- **Outcome:** Increases operational efficiency and enhances decision-making with accurate, data-driven insights.

14.4.2 Implementing Circular Economy Principles

A circular economy minimizes waste and maximizes the reuse of materials, products, and resources. By transitioning to circular business models, organisations can reduce their dependence on finite resources, improve efficiency, and build greater resilience against supply chain disruptions.

- **Actionable Practice:** Develop strategies to reduce, reuse, and recycle materials within the production process, and establish closed-loop systems for product life cycles.
- **Outcome:** Reduces waste, improves material efficiency, and strengthens the overall resilience of the organisation's operations.

14.5 Case Studies: Businesses Demonstrating Resilience

14.5.1 Case Study: Patagonia and Climate Resilience

Patagonia is known for its commitment to sustainability and environmental stewardship. The company has long been at the forefront of resilience strategies, focusing not only on reducing its own carbon footprint but also on adapting to the impacts of climate change. Patagonia's use of renewable energy in its operations and its emphasis on sustainable sourcing have made it a leader in environmental resilience.

- **Actionable Practice:** Incorporate sustainable business models that align with your core values, while also investing in resilience strategies that address climate risk and supply chain vulnerabilities.

- **Outcome:** Drives long-term value creation through sustainable innovation and adaptation to environmental challenges.

14.5.2 Case Study: Unilever's Sustainable Supply Chain

Unilever, a global leader in consumer goods, has Prioritised building resilience into its supply chain. By diversifying suppliers, implementing sustainability criteria for sourcing, and investing in renewable energy, Unilever has been able to ensure that its operations remain resilient in the face of climate and supply chain disruptions.

- **Actionable Practice:** Develop sustainable procurement policies, diversify your supply chain, and engage suppliers on environmental and social issues to enhance resilience.

- **Outcome:** Strengthens long-term business operations while reducing exposure to climate and supply chain risks.

14.6 Conclusion: Preparing for the Future with Resilience and Adaptability

As organisations continue to navigate the complex landscape of climate change and sustainability, the need for resilient and adaptive strategies will only grow. By embracing proactive climate action, leveraging technology, engaging stakeholders, and fostering collaboration, businesses can build the resilience necessary to thrive in an uncertain world.

Chapter 15: Communicating Sustainability and Resilience to Stakeholders

Effective communication is one of the most crucial elements in implementing and sustaining a successful sustainability and resilience strategy. In this chapter, we will explore how businesses can communicate their sustainability and resilience initiatives, challenges, and successes to stakeholders, ensuring alignment with their values and engaging them in meaningful ways. The ability to transparently convey sustainability efforts helps reinforce trust, fosters long-term partnerships, and ensures continued support from all stakeholders, including employees, investors, customers, and communities.

15.1 Why Communication is Key to Sustainability Success

15.1.1 The Role of Communication in Sustainability

Communicating sustainability efforts allows businesses to share their vision, progress, and commitment to stakeholders. Well-executed communication efforts help align stakeholders with the organisation's sustainability goals, making them feel more involved in the process and more willing to support the business. It also ensures that any challenges or setbacks are openly addressed, fostering a sense of transparency and accountability.

For businesses, sustainability communication isn't just about highlighting successes; it also involves engaging with stakeholders during difficult times to show a genuine commitment to overcoming challenges and improving future strategies.

- **Actionable Practice:** Develop a communication strategy that includes regular updates, both positive and negative, to keep stakeholders informed and involved in the business's sustainability journey.
- **Outcome:** Builds a strong sense of transparency and credibility among stakeholders, strengthening relationships and supporting long-term commitment to sustainability.

15.1.2 The Importance of Transparency in Sustainability Reporting

Transparency is one of the pillars of effective communication in sustainability. By providing clear, concise, and honest reporting, businesses demonstrate their commitment to accountability. Transparent communication also aligns with industry standards and expectations, including frameworks such as the **Global Reporting Initiative (GRI)**, **Task Force on Climate-related Financial Disclosures (TCFD)**, and **Sustainable Development Goals (SDGs)**.

- **Actionable Practice:** Use recognised reporting frameworks like GRI, TCFD, and others to disclose the organisation's sustainability efforts, climate risks, and performance against defined goals.

- **Outcome:** Positions the organization as a credible and responsible actor in the sustainability space, earning the trust of investors, customers, and regulatory bodies.

15.2 Key Strategies for Effective Communication

15.2.1 Tailor the Message for Different Audiences

Different stakeholders have varying levels of interest and understanding of sustainability issues. Some stakeholders, such as investors, may require in-depth data on climate risks, while consumers may be more interested in the ethical sourcing of products. It's important to tailor the messaging to meet the needs and expectations of each group.

- **Actionable Practice:** Develop specific communication campaigns for each stakeholder group (employees, customers, investors, communities) and adjust the complexity of the message to suit their interests.

- **Outcome:** Engages each group in a manner that resonates with their values and knowledge, ensuring that sustainability messages are both informative and impactful.

15.2.2 Leverage Digital Platforms for Broader Reach

In today's digital age, social media, websites, blogs, and other online platforms are indispensable tools for communicating sustainability efforts. By using these platforms, businesses can reach a wider audience, share real-time updates, and invite public participation in sustainability initiatives. These platforms also allow for instant feedback, helping organisations quickly gauge public sentiment and make necessary adjustments.

- **Actionable Practice:** Utilize digital platforms to regularly update stakeholders on sustainability progress, share success stories, and engage the public in discussions about sustainability.

- **Outcome:** Expands the reach of sustainability initiatives and enhances engagement through real-time interactions and feedback.

15.2.3 Storytelling: Connecting Emotionally with Stakeholders

While facts, data, and numbers are important, stories have the power to engage people on an emotional level. By sharing personal stories about how sustainability efforts have positively impacted employees, communities, and the environment, businesses can connect more deeply with their audience. Storytelling makes sustainability efforts relatable and shows the tangible benefits of the company's work.

- **Actionable Practice:** Share compelling stories of employees, community members, or local organisations benefiting from sustainability programs, whether through employment, education, or environmental improvement.

- **Outcome:** Inspires stakeholders and reinforces the business's commitment to social and environmental impact.

15.3 Addressing Challenges and Setbacks with Integrity

15.3.1 Acknowledging and Addressing Challenges

While celebrating successes is important, acknowledging challenges or setbacks is equally critical. Communicating challenges openly with stakeholders allows businesses to build trust. It shows that the organization is aware of the difficulties it faces and is taking steps to address them. Whether it's struggling to meet certain environmental goals or facing regulatory changes, transparency about obstacles creates credibility.

- **Actionable Practice:** Be upfront about challenges and setbacks in sustainability efforts. Share the steps being taken to overcome these obstacles and the timeline for addressing them.

- **Outcome:** Demonstrates resilience and integrity, turning setbacks into opportunities for growth and improvement.

15.3.2 Providing Clear and Actionable Solutions

Simply identifying challenges is not enough; businesses need to provide solutions. Stakeholders want to know what is being done to resolve issues and how they can contribute. Offering actionable solutions to overcome challenges or accelerate progress strengthens the organisation's reputation as a problem solver.

- **Actionable Practice:** Provide clear, actionable plans outlining how the business intends to overcome challenges, such as adjusting emissions reduction targets or improving community engagement.
- **Outcome:** Reinforces the organisation's ability to adapt and stay committed to its sustainability goals despite obstacles.

15.4 Measurement and Reporting: Demonstrating Progress

15.4.1 Establishing Clear Metrics

To show stakeholders that sustainability initiatives are having a meaningful impact, businesses must track and report on key metrics. These metrics can include carbon emissions, water usage, waste reduction, employee engagement in sustainability programs, or progress on diversity and inclusion goals. Setting clear, measurable goals is essential for providing transparency.

- **Actionable Practice:** Set specific, measurable targets for each aspect of sustainability—environmental, social, and governance—and track progress regularly.
- **Outcome:** Provides tangible evidence of sustainability efforts and allows businesses to showcase progress over time.

15.4.2 Using Visuals and Data to Support Reporting

Data and visuals are powerful tools in communicating sustainability progress. Infographics, graphs, and charts can present complex information in a digestible format that is easy for stakeholders to understand. This is particularly useful when reporting on emissions reductions, water conservation, or energy efficiency.

- **Actionable Practice:** Incorporate visuals into sustainability reports to highlight key achievements and trends, making it easier for stakeholders to interpret the data.

- **Outcome:** Increases the clarity of communication and ensures that stakeholders can quickly grasp the organisation's sustainability performance.

15.5 Case Study: Effective Communication in Action

15.5.1 Case Study: Unilever's Transparency in Sustainability Reporting

Unilever has been a leader in sustainability reporting, consistently providing transparent updates on its sustainability goals, achievements, and challenges. Their reports include comprehensive data, clear visuals, and measurable targets, which have helped the company build trust with its customers, investors, and partners.

- **Actionable Practice:** Develop detailed sustainability reports with transparent data and clear visuals to keep stakeholders informed about your progress.

- **Outcome:** Establishes credibility and trust, positioning the organization as a transparent and accountable entity in the sustainability space.

15.5.2 Case Study: Patagonia's Storytelling Approach

Patagonia has successfully used storytelling to connect with its customers and stakeholders. Through compelling narratives about environmental activism, their products' journey, and the positive impacts of their sustainability efforts, Patagonia has fostered deep emotional connections with consumers.

- **Actionable Practice:** Share powerful stories of how your sustainability efforts are changing lives and benefiting communities.

- **Outcome:** Engages stakeholders on an emotional level, inspiring them to take action and support your initiatives.

15.6 Conclusion: The Power of Communication in Building Trust and Engagement

In this chapter, we explored how effective communication is essential for building trust, engaging stakeholders, and driving the success of sustainability strategies. Whether it's through transparent reporting, sharing challenges, or telling compelling stories, businesses can foster stronger relationships with their stakeholders and demonstrate their long-term commitment to sustainability and resilience.

Chapter 16: The Future of Sustainability: Emerging Trends and Innovations

As businesses continue to embrace sustainability and align with global environmental, social, and governance (ESG) goals, it is essential to look to the future. Emerging trends, innovative technologies, and evolving business models are set to shape the future of sustainability in profound ways. In this chapter, we will explore these future trends and how businesses can harness these opportunities to stay ahead of the curve, contribute to global sustainability efforts, and create long-term value.

16.1 The Rise of Green Innovation and Technological Solutions

16.1.1 Innovations in Renewable Energy

The transition to renewable energy has been one of the most impactful and transformative trends in recent years. As technology continues to evolve, the cost of renewable energy, such as solar, wind, and hydropower, has significantly decreased, making it increasingly accessible for businesses across industries. However, the future of sustainability goes beyond just adopting renewable energy—it's about integrating new innovations into energy systems that are smarter, more efficient, and more resilient.

- **Actionable Practice:** Invest in emerging energy technologies, such as **smart grids**, **energy storage systems**, and **hybrid renewable systems**, to ensure a reliable, flexible, and sustainable energy supply.

- **Outcome:** Reduces carbon footprints, lowers energy costs, and prepares businesses for a future driven by renewable energy solutions.

16.1.2 The Role of Artificial Intelligence and Big Data in Sustainability

Artificial intelligence (AI) and big data have already begun revolutionizing the way businesses approach sustainability. From optimizing supply chains and predicting climate-related risks to improving resource management and reducing energy consumption, AI and big data have vast potential to enhance sustainability efforts. By analysing vast amounts of data, AI can identify patterns and recommend solutions that might otherwise go unnoticed.

- **Actionable Practice:** Implement AI-powered tools to monitor and optimise energy consumption, track waste, predict supply chain disruptions, and optimise resource usage.

- **Outcome:** Drives operational efficiency, reduces waste, and enhances sustainability performance through data-driven insights.

16.1.3 Blockchain for Supply Chain Transparency

Blockchain technology offers a powerful tool for improving transparency and accountability in supply chains. By using blockchain, businesses can track the movement of goods and materials from origin to end consumer, ensuring that sustainability standards are being met at every stage. This technology can help combat unethical practices, such as sourcing from non-sustainable suppliers or engaging in labor violations.

- **Actionable Practice:** Invest in blockchain-based systems to provide full transparency in your supply chain and ensure that all suppliers adhere to your sustainability and ethical standards.

- **Outcome:** Strengthens brand credibility, ensures compliance with sustainability standards, and builds trust among consumers, investors, and other stakeholders.

16.2 Circular Economy: A New Model for Sustainable Growth

16.2.1 The Shift Towards a Circular Economy

The traditional linear economy model—take, make, dispose—has led to unsustainable resource consumption, excessive waste, and environmental degradation. The circular economy, however, focuses on closing the loop by designing products and systems that minimize waste, promote reuse, and extend the lifecycle of materials. In the future, businesses will increasingly adopt circular principles across their operations to reduce environmental impacts and create new value streams.

- **Actionable Practice:** Design products with longer life cycles, implement take-back schemes for product recycling, and partner with recycling organisations to close the loop.

- **Outcome:** Reduces reliance on virgin resources, minimizes waste, and opens up new business opportunities by creating sustainable product life cycles.

16.2.2 Business Models for a Circular Economy

Circular business models focus on value creation while minimizing environmental harm. These models include product-as-a-service offerings, where customers lease products instead of purchasing them, allowing companies to retain ownership and responsibility for repair, reuse, and recycling. Other models involve remanufacturing, upcycling, and refurbishing products to keep them in use for longer periods.

- **Actionable Practice:** Shift to service-based models where appropriate, such as offering products as a service or establishing a product take-back program to enable recycling and reuse.

- **Outcome:** Maximizes the value of materials, minimizes waste, and aligns business practices with sustainable economic systems.

16.3 The Role of Green Finance and Investment

16.3.1 Green Bonds and Sustainability-Linked Loans

As the demand for sustainable finance grows, more companies and governments are issuing green bonds and sustainability-linked loans to fund environmental projects and initiatives. These financial instruments allow businesses to raise capital for initiatives that will reduce environmental impacts, such as renewable energy projects or sustainable infrastructure development. The growth of green finance is set to continue, offering a key opportunity for businesses to access funding for their sustainability efforts.

- **Actionable Practice:** Explore opportunities to issue green bonds or seek sustainability-linked loans to finance renewable energy projects, sustainable building initiatives, or other climate-resilient infrastructure.

- **Outcome:** Facilitates access to capital for sustainability projects, supports long-term growth, and demonstrates a commitment to reducing environmental impact.

16.3.2 The Growing Role of Impact Investing

Impact investing focuses on generating measurable positive social and environmental outcomes alongside financial returns. This form of investing is becoming more popular among institutional investors, who increasingly seek to align their portfolios with the SDGs. Impact investing offers businesses a unique opportunity to attract funding for projects that drive both financial and sustainability performance.

- **Actionable Practice:** Seek impact investors who share your commitment to sustainability and social responsibility, and align your projects with measurable environmental and social outcomes.

- **Outcome:** Accesses funding for projects that promote sustainable development and contributes to a positive social impact.

16.4 Policy and Regulatory Trends Shaping the Future of Sustainability

16.4.1 Stricter Environmental Regulations

Governments worldwide are increasingly implementing stricter regulations to combat climate change and protect ecosystems. These regulations may include carbon pricing, emission reduction targets, mandatory sustainability disclosures, and restrictions on resource extraction. As these policies evolve, businesses will need to adapt to meet regulatory requirements and avoid financial penalties.

- **Actionable Practice:** Stay informed about upcoming regulations in your industry and proactively adopt practices that align with anticipated policy changes, such as reducing emissions or increasing transparency in sustainability reporting.

- **Outcome:** Minimizes the risk of non-compliance and positions the organization as a leader in sustainability.

16.4.2 Global Climate Agreements and Commitments

International agreements, such as the Paris Agreement, play a central role in shaping the future of sustainability. Businesses will need to align their operations with global climate targets and commitments, ensuring they contribute to achieving net-zero emissions and sustainable development goals. Global collaborations and climate summits will continue to influence national and local policies, driving further commitment to sustainability.

- **Actionable Practice:** Align your sustainability goals with global climate agreements and actively participate in international initiatives aimed at addressing climate change.

- **Outcome:** Supports the global push towards sustainability and ensures your business remains in compliance with international agreements.

16.5 Preparing for the Future: How to Stay Ahead

16.5.1 Foster Innovation and Experimentation

The future of sustainability will be driven by innovation. Businesses that foster a culture of experimentation and innovation, supported by research and development, will be better positioned to adapt to future sustainability challenges. This includes developing new products, services, or technologies that address unmet environmental or social needs.

- **Actionable Practice:** Create an innovation lab or dedicate resources to research and development aimed at finding sustainable solutions in areas such as materials science, energy efficiency, and waste management.

- **Outcome:** Positions your business as a leader in sustainability innovation and ensures future adaptability.

16.5.2 Build Resilience into Operations

The future is unpredictable, and climate-related risks, such as extreme weather, will continue to pose challenges. Businesses that build resilience into their operations, such as diversifying supply chains, enhancing energy efficiency, and investing in climate-proof infrastructure, will be better equipped to withstand disruptions and maintain operations in the face of adversity.

- **Actionable Practice:** Incorporate climate resilience planning into your business strategy, including supply chain diversification, disaster recovery planning, and climate-proof infrastructure.

- **Outcome:** Enhances your business's ability to recover quickly from disruptions, ensuring long-term sustainability.

16.6 Conclusion: The Road Ahead

The future of sustainability is full of opportunities, innovations, and challenges. As businesses continue to navigate this evolving landscape, adopting emerging technologies, aligning with global climate commitments, and embracing new business models will be essential to staying competitive and responsible. By preparing for the future today, businesses not only contribute to global sustainability goals but also secure their long-term viability and success in an increasingly environmentally conscious world.

Chapter 17: Leadership for Sustainability: Driving Change from the Top

In the face of mounting environmental and social challenges, businesses need leaders who can inspire and drive meaningful change. Leadership plays a critical role in determining the pace, direction, and success of sustainability initiatives within organisations. This chapter will explore how business leaders can shape the future of sustainability, lead their organisations through complex challenges, and create a culture that aligns with long-term sustainable goals.

17.1 The Role of Leadership in Sustainability

17.1.1 Leading by Example

The most effective leaders in sustainability don't just talk about the importance of environmental responsibility—they actively demonstrate it in their actions. Leading by example means making tough decisions, integrating sustainability into all aspects of business operations, and setting measurable goals for environmental performance. Leadership on sustainability is about creating a clear vision, setting ambitious targets, and remaining accountable for achieving them.

- **Actionable Practice:** Commit to reducing your own environmental footprint as a leader. Adopt sustainable business practices such as reducing personal emissions, using energy-efficient modes of transport, or switching to renewable energy sources at the company headquarters.

- **Outcome:** Establishes credibility and shows employees, customers, and stakeholders that sustainability is not just a priority for the organization but is embedded in its leadership culture.

17.1.2 Creating a Shared Vision for Sustainability

Successful sustainability initiatives start with a shared vision. Leaders must clearly articulate a vision of sustainability that resonates with employees, investors, customers, and partners. This vision should align with the company's overall mission, be backed by measurable goals, and address the environmental, social, and economic impacts of the business. A shared vision enables stakeholders to work toward the same set of outcomes, making collaboration and action more effective.

- **Actionable Practice:** Organize workshops and meetings with key stakeholders to develop a shared sustainability vision. Ensure that this vision is embedded in the company's mission and values.

- **Outcome:** Aligns the entire organization behind a common goal, creating cohesion, motivation, and focus in driving sustainability efforts.

17.1.3 Championing Corporate Social Responsibility (CSR)

As sustainability becomes an integral part of business success, corporate social responsibility (CSR) is no longer a peripheral activity. Leaders must champion CSR as a core business function and drive its integration into all departments. By making CSR a priority, leaders can transform their companies into engines of social and environmental change.

- **Actionable Practice:** Invest in sustainable development projects, ensure fair labor practices in your supply chain, and make substantial investments in your local community.

- **Outcome:** Demonstrates the company's commitment to addressing societal and environmental issues, fostering goodwill, and making a tangible difference in the community.

17.2 Fostering a Culture of Sustainability within the Organization

17.2.1 Building Employee Engagement

Sustainability efforts will not succeed without the active involvement of employees. Leaders must create an organizational culture where sustainability is embedded in the core values, where employees at all levels are empowered to contribute to environmental goals, and where sustainability is rewarded and recognised. An engaged workforce is more likely to contribute innovative ideas and champion sustainability initiatives.

- **Actionable Practice:** Establish employee sustainability committees, incentivise eco-friendly behavior, and include sustainability goals in employee performance reviews.

- **Outcome:** Fosters a sense of ownership, accountability, and pride in employees, resulting in higher engagement and more successful sustainability outcomes.

17.2.2 Training and Development for Sustainability

Leaders should provide ongoing training and professional development opportunities to ensure that employees understand the importance of sustainability and how it applies to their roles. This includes providing knowledge about sustainability risks, opportunities, and best practices across the value chain. An informed workforce will be better equipped to make decisions that align with the company's sustainability goals.

- **Actionable Practice:** Develop and implement a comprehensive training program focused on sustainability, climate change, and social responsibility, with a focus on the relevance of sustainability to each department's work.

- **Outcome:** Empowers employees with the knowledge and skills needed to contribute to the organisation's sustainability efforts, leading to better decision-making and more innovative solutions.

17.2.3 Promoting Diversity and Inclusion in Sustainability Leadership

A truly sustainable organization is one that includes diverse perspectives, particularly in its leadership. Diversity of thought, background, and experience is essential for developing innovative solutions to environmental and social challenges. By promoting diverse representation at all levels of the organization, including leadership roles, companies can better tackle complex sustainability issues and improve outcomes.

- **Actionable Practice:** Establish diversity, equity, and inclusion (DEI) initiatives to promote diverse leadership within sustainability and other key departments.

- **Outcome:** Strengthens decision-making processes, improves social responsibility, and ensures that the company is well-positioned to meet the needs of a diverse customer base and global community.

17.3 The Strategic Business Case for Sustainability

17.3.1 Financial Performance and Risk Management

In the past, sustainability was often seen as a cost center—something that businesses needed to do out of goodwill or corporate responsibility. However, this view is changing. Sustainability is now widely recognised as a driver of financial performance. By reducing waste, improving resource efficiency, and minimizing risks associated with climate change, businesses can realize significant cost savings and open up new revenue streams. Sustainable practices also mitigate risks associated with resource scarcity, regulation, and climate change, providing a long-term financial advantage.

- **Actionable Practice:** Integrate sustainability into risk management by evaluating potential environmental and regulatory risks and developing strategies to mitigate these.

- **Outcome:** Reduces operational risks, improves financial performance, and ensures long-term profitability and viability.

17.3.2 Enhancing Brand Reputation and Customer Loyalty

Leaders who embrace sustainability will find that it strengthens their brand reputation and deepens customer loyalty. Consumers are increasingly looking for businesses that Prioritise environmental responsibility, ethical labor practices, and social justice. By leading with integrity and demonstrating a genuine commitment to sustainability, companies can differentiate themselves in the marketplace and build strong, lasting relationships with customers.

- **Actionable Practice:** Promote your sustainability efforts through marketing campaigns, certifications (e.g., B Corp), and transparent reporting.

- **Outcome:** Strengthens the company's brand and fosters customer loyalty, ultimately driving sales and market share.

17.3.3 Partnering with Stakeholders for Broader Impact

Effective sustainability leadership involves collaboration, not just within the organization but with external stakeholders as well. Companies can leverage partnerships with governments, NGOs, industry peers, and local communities to drive broader change.

These collaborations can result in innovative solutions to sustainability challenges and open up opportunities for new markets and projects.

- **Actionable Practice:** Build strategic partnerships with like-minded organisations, stakeholders, and sustainability-focused initiatives.

- **Outcome:** Extends the impact of sustainability efforts, promotes knowledge sharing, and accelerates the achievement of environmental and social goals.

17.4 Conclusion: Leaders as Catalysts for a Sustainable Future

Leadership in sustainability requires vision, commitment, and action. As the world faces unprecedented environmental and social challenges, the role of business leaders in driving change has never been more critical. By fostering a culture of sustainability, engaging employees, aligning business strategies with sustainable goals, and driving ethical practices, leaders can shape a future that is resilient, equitable, and sustainable. Through their actions, business leaders not only contribute to the global sustainability movement but also secure long-term value and success for their organisations.

Chapter 18: Integrating ESG and Biodiversity into Business Strategies

As businesses navigate the complex landscape of environmental, social, and governance (ESG) factors, they increasingly face the challenge of integrating biodiversity into their strategies. Biodiversity loss poses significant risks to ecosystems, human well-being, and the economy, making it essential for businesses to incorporate biodiversity considerations into their ESG frameworks. This chapter will explore how organisations can align their operations with biodiversity goals, mitigate risks, and contribute to the global effort to protect biodiversity.

18.1 Understanding the Business Case for Biodiversity

18.1.1 The Role of Biodiversity in Business

Biodiversity supports healthy ecosystems, which in turn provide essential services such as clean water, air, soil fertility, and climate regulation. These ecosystem services are vital to the continuity of business operations across sectors such as agriculture, construction, tourism, and pharmaceuticals. However, the degradation of biodiversity can disrupt supply chains, increase operational risks, and damage a company's reputation. As a result, businesses must acknowledge their direct and indirect dependencies on biodiversity and take proactive steps to protect it.

- **Actionable Practice:** Identify and assess the dependencies and impacts of your operations on local ecosystems and biodiversity.
- **Outcome:** Recognising biodiversity as a core business risk and opportunity, driving more informed decision-making and sustainable business practices.

18.1.2 Biodiversity Risks and Opportunities

Businesses face both risks and opportunities related to biodiversity. Risks include regulatory changes, reputational damage, and supply chain disruptions caused by biodiversity loss. Conversely, businesses that integrate biodiversity into their operations can unlock new opportunities, such as innovative product development, improved resource efficiency, and access to new markets. Moreover, companies that engage in biodiversity conservation efforts can differentiate themselves as sustainability leaders, enhancing their market position.

- **Actionable Practice:** Conduct a biodiversity risk assessment and engage stakeholders to identify opportunities for positive impact.
- **Outcome:** Reduces exposure to risks associated with biodiversity loss and positions the company as a responsible and forward-thinking entity.

18.2 Incorporating Biodiversity into ESG Strategies

18.2.1 Setting Clear Biodiversity Goals

Integrating biodiversity into business strategies requires clear, actionable goals. These goals should be specific, measurable, achievable, relevant, and time-bound (SMART) and aligned with both global frameworks like the Convention on Biological Diversity (CBD) and the business's specific operational context. Whether the goal is to reduce the company's environmental footprint, protect local ecosystems, or support biodiversity conservation efforts, setting targets is crucial to driving progress and accountability.

- **Actionable Practice:** Establish biodiversity-specific targets and integrate them into the company's overarching ESG strategy.
- **Outcome:** Provides clear direction for biodiversity initiatives and ensures that progress can be tracked and measured.

18.2.2 Aligning with Global Biodiversity Standards

Several international frameworks and standards provide guidance on how to integrate biodiversity into business operations. These include the CBD, the Global Reporting Initiative (GRI) standards, and the Task Force on Nature-related Financial Disclosures (TNFD). Adhering to these standards helps businesses align their biodiversity efforts with global best practices and ensures transparency and consistency in reporting.

- **Actionable Practice:** Adopt internationally recognised biodiversity reporting standards and incorporate them into your company's sustainability reports.
- **Outcome:** Demonstrates a commitment to global biodiversity goals and builds trust with stakeholders, including investors, regulators, and the public.

18.2.3 Mainstreaming Biodiversity in Decision-Making

Biodiversity should be incorporated into the decision-making process at all levels of the organization. This involves ensuring that biodiversity is considered when making strategic, operational, and investment decisions. Businesses should consider the long-term implications of their actions on ecosystems and incorporate biodiversity considerations into their risk management, procurement, and product development processes.

- **Actionable Practice:** Integrate biodiversity assessments into key decision-making processes, including capital investments, product design, and supply chain management.
- **Outcome:** Ensures that the company's operations are not inadvertently contributing to biodiversity loss, while also identifying opportunities for positive impact.

18.3 Building Partnerships for Biodiversity Conservation

18.3.1 Collaborating with Conservation Organisations

Many businesses are now partnering with conservation organisations, NGOs, and local communities to actively protect and restore biodiversity. These partnerships can range from supporting biodiversity-focused conservation projects to co-developing innovative solutions that promote sustainable land and water use. Collaborative efforts help businesses leverage external expertise, access funding opportunities, and enhance their impact.

- **Actionable Practice:** Build partnerships with local and global conservation organisations, such as WWF, The Nature Conservancy, or local environmental NGOs.
- **Outcome:** Expands the reach and impact of biodiversity efforts and strengthens relationships with key stakeholders.

18.3.2 Supporting Community-Led Biodiversity Initiatives

Incorporating local communities' knowledge and expertise into biodiversity conservation efforts is crucial. Many indigenous communities have a long-standing relationship with the land and possess valuable traditional knowledge about sustainable resource management and ecosystem preservation. By supporting these community-led initiatives, businesses can enhance their sustainability efforts, promote social responsibility, and empower local communities.

- **Actionable Practice:** Partner with Indigenous communities and other local stakeholders to support community-led biodiversity conservation projects.
- **Outcome:** Empowers local communities, fosters inclusive development, and ensures that biodiversity efforts are culturally appropriate and grounded in local knowledge.

18.4 Measuring and Reporting Biodiversity Performance

18.4.1 Establishing Biodiversity Metrics

As with any sustainability initiative, businesses must measure and report on their biodiversity performance to ensure accountability. This includes tracking key biodiversity indicators, such as species richness, habitat quality, and ecosystem services. Monitoring biodiversity performance allows companies to gauge the effectiveness of their conservation strategies and adjust them as necessary.

- **Actionable Practice:** Develop key performance indicators (KPIs) for biodiversity, including direct and indirect impacts, and integrate these into the company's sustainability reporting framework.
- **Outcome:** Provides measurable data on biodiversity impacts and ensures continuous improvement in conservation efforts.

18.4.2 Transparent Biodiversity Reporting

Transparency in biodiversity reporting is crucial for building trust with stakeholders, including investors, customers, and regulatory bodies. Businesses should provide detailed information on their biodiversity impacts, strategies, and progress, and align their reports with international standards, such as the Global Reporting Initiative (GRI) and the Integrated Reporting Framework.

- **Actionable Practice:** Publish annual sustainability reports that include detailed information on biodiversity initiatives, progress, and challenges.

- **Outcome:** Enhances the company's credibility and demonstrates its commitment to protecting biodiversity.

18.5 Conclusion: The Path Forward for Biodiversity in Business

Incorporating biodiversity into business strategies is not just a moral obligation—it's a strategic advantage. Companies that Prioritise biodiversity conservation not only contribute to global sustainability goals but also position themselves for long-term success by mitigating risks, reducing costs, and building stronger relationships with stakeholders. The journey towards integrating biodiversity into business practices requires collaboration, commitment, and continuous improvement, but the rewards are significant for both the business and the planet.

Chapter 19: Engaging Stakeholders in Biodiversity and ESG Efforts

In this chapter, we will explore how businesses can actively engage stakeholders in their biodiversity and environmental, social, and governance (ESG) efforts. Engaging stakeholders is critical to ensuring the success of sustainability initiatives, fostering transparency, and building meaningful relationships that benefit both the business and the wider community. Effective engagement also allows businesses to understand stakeholder concerns and expectations, which can inform strategy and improve overall outcomes.

19.1 The Importance of Stakeholder Engagement in Biodiversity Conservation

19.1.1 Understanding the Role of Stakeholders

Stakeholders are individuals or groups who are affected by or can affect a company's operations, products, and sustainability efforts. In the context of biodiversity and ESG, stakeholders can include a wide range of actors such as employees, customers, suppliers, investors, local communities, environmental NGOs, and government agencies. Engaging these stakeholders ensures that the business is not only addressing their concerns but also benefiting from their insights, expertise, and support.

Stakeholder engagement helps to:

- Build trust and credibility.

- Identify risks and opportunities.

- Strengthen community and customer loyalty.

- Enhance environmental performance through collaborative efforts.

- **Actionable Practice:** Create a stakeholder mapping process to identify key individuals and groups with an interest in biodiversity and ESG initiatives.

- **Outcome:** Ensures that the business understands its diverse stakeholder landscape and can tailor its engagement efforts accordingly.

19.1.2 Types of Stakeholders and Their Interests

- **Internal Stakeholders** (e.g., employees, management):
    - Employees are a critical part of the business's efforts to promote sustainability. Their engagement ensures alignment with company goals, facilitates the implementation of sustainable practices, and boosts morale.
    - Management plays a key role in setting the strategic direction and fostering a sustainability culture within the organization.
- **External Stakeholders** (e.g., investors, customers, suppliers, local communities, NGOs):
    - Investors are increasingly prioritising ESG factors, including biodiversity. They seek assurance that companies are addressing environmental risks and contributing positively to sustainability goals.
    - Customers are becoming more aware of environmental issues, and many prefer to support companies that demonstrate commitment to sustainable practices.
    - Suppliers are essential for ensuring the sustainability of the supply chain. Engaging suppliers on biodiversity goals and ethical practices is vital for fostering responsible sourcing and reducing negative environmental impacts.
    - Local communities and NGOs can offer valuable knowledge and resources, particularly when it comes to biodiversity conservation, land stewardship, and environmental restoration.
- **Actionable Practice:** Develop targeted engagement strategies for different stakeholder groups based on their unique interests and concerns.
- **Outcome:** Ensures that engagement efforts are effective, relevant, and beneficial to all parties involved.

19.2 Strategies for Effective Stakeholder Engagement

19.2.1 Transparent Communication

Transparency is key in building trust and credibility with stakeholders. Businesses should openly share their biodiversity-related goals, strategies, challenges, and progress. Providing stakeholders with accurate, timely, and clear information ensures they feel informed and involved in the company's efforts.

- **Actionable Practice:** Regularly update stakeholders through sustainability reports, newsletters, and dedicated meetings about biodiversity-related initiatives and outcomes.
- **Outcome:** Strengthens relationships with stakeholders and demonstrates accountability.

19.2.2 Collaborative Partnerships

One of the most effective ways to engage stakeholders is through collaboration. Partnering with local communities, environmental NGOs, and other businesses allows for a shared approach to solving complex environmental problems. Joint efforts can amplify the impact of biodiversity conservation initiatives, pool resources, and ensure alignment with local and global sustainability goals.

- **Actionable Practice:** Form strategic partnerships with conservation organisations, community groups, and academic institutions to co-develop biodiversity programs.
- **Outcome:** Enhances the impact of biodiversity efforts and ensures that the business is leveraging external expertise and resources effectively.

19.2.3 Stakeholder Dialogues and Consultations

Engaging in dialogues and consultations with stakeholders provides valuable insights into their concerns and expectations. These interactions can help businesses identify potential risks, improve their sustainability efforts, and gain support for biodiversity initiatives.

- **Actionable Practice:** Host stakeholder consultations, town hall meetings, and focus groups to gather feedback on biodiversity strategies and programs.
- **Outcome:** Fosters stronger relationships with stakeholders and ensures that their input is considered in the decision-making process.

19.3 Addressing Concerns and Building Support for Biodiversity Efforts

19.3.1 Addressing Stakeholder Concerns

Stakeholders may have varying levels of knowledge and interest in biodiversity conservation. While some may be passionate advocates, others might not see biodiversity as a priority. Addressing concerns proactively is essential to ensuring continued support. Businesses should listen to stakeholder feedback, address misunderstandings, and clarify the long-term benefits of protecting biodiversity.

- **Actionable Practice:** Provide stakeholders with clear, compelling evidence of the business's positive impact on biodiversity, such as case studies, research data, and success stories.
- **Outcome:** Reduces skepticism and garners stakeholder support for biodiversity initiatives.

19.3.2 Creating Shared Value

One of the most powerful ways to engage stakeholders is by demonstrating how biodiversity initiatives can create shared value. Businesses that align their sustainability efforts with the needs of local communities, biodiversity, and the broader environment create positive social, environmental, and economic outcomes for all stakeholders.

- **Actionable Practice:** Highlight the direct and indirect benefits of biodiversity efforts to local communities, such as job creation, improved ecosystem services, and enhanced quality of life.
- **Outcome:** Strengthens community relations and secures broader support for biodiversity efforts.

19.4 Conclusion: Strengthening Biodiversity Engagement for Long-Term Success

Stakeholder engagement is not just about addressing concerns; it's about creating a collaborative and inclusive environment where everyone feels involved and valued. By aligning biodiversity goals with stakeholder interests, businesses can achieve greater impact, mitigate risks, and ensure that their sustainability efforts are truly effective. This collaborative approach will ultimately help businesses build stronger relationships, contribute to global biodiversity conservation goals, and achieve long-term success.

Chapter 20: Measuring and Reporting the Impact of Biodiversity Initiatives

In this chapter, we will explore how businesses can effectively measure and report the impact of their biodiversity and environmental, social, and governance (ESG) initiatives. Measuring progress is crucial for understanding whether the goals are being met, identifying areas for improvement, and maintaining transparency with stakeholders. Effective reporting not only enhances accountability but also drives continuous improvement, allowing businesses to refine their strategies and achieve long-term sustainability.

20.1 The Importance of Measuring Biodiversity Impact

20.1.1 Why Measuring Biodiversity is Essential

Biodiversity is often considered a complex and intangible concept, making it difficult for companies to assess and measure their impacts. However, measuring biodiversity is critical for businesses to understand the direct and indirect effects of their operations on ecosystems and species. Without proper measurement, businesses cannot evaluate the effectiveness of their efforts or identify opportunities to reduce negative impacts.

Key reasons why measuring biodiversity is important:

- **Accountability:** Provides transparency on how business operations impact the environment.

- **Performance Evaluation:** Allows businesses to assess whether their sustainability initiatives are delivering the desired results.

- **Stakeholder Engagement:** Demonstrates the organisation's commitment to biodiversity and sustainability goals to stakeholders.

- **Risk Management:** Helps identify biodiversity-related risks that could affect the business, such as loss of natural resources or reputation damage.

- **Actionable Practice:** Establish a biodiversity measurement framework aligned with international standards and tools, such as the Global Reporting Initiative (GRI) or the Natural Capital Protocol.

- **Outcome:** Provides a structured approach for tracking and reporting biodiversity metrics effectively.

20.1.2 Types of Biodiversity Metrics

There are various types of biodiversity metrics that businesses can use to assess their impact. These metrics typically fall into the following categories:

- **Ecological Footprint:** Measures the total land and water area required to produce resources used by the business and absorb its waste.

- **Biodiversity Indices:** Commonly used indices include the Biodiversity Intactness Index (BII), which measures the condition of ecosystems, and the Red List Index (RLI), which assesses the extinction risk of species.

- **Species Count and Habitat Quality:** Tracks the number of species in a specific area and the health or quality of their habitats.

- **Carbon Sequestration Potential:** Measures the capacity of ecosystems to absorb and store carbon dioxide.

- **Water Use and Pollution:** Measures the impact of the business's water use, including any pollution or contamination of local water bodies.

- **Actionable Practice:** Choose the most relevant biodiversity metrics based on the business's operations, location, and sustainability goals.

- **Outcome:** Aligns biodiversity measurement with the company's specific impact and objectives.

20.2 Methods for Measuring Biodiversity Impact

20.2.1 Baseline Assessments and Data Collection

Before businesses can measure their impact on biodiversity, they need to understand the current state of the ecosystems and habitats in the areas where they operate. Baseline assessments involve gathering data on species, habitats, and environmental conditions to establish a starting point for future comparisons. This data will be essential for evaluating how business activities influence local biodiversity.

- **Actionable Practice:** Conduct initial biodiversity assessments through partnerships with conservation experts, scientists, or local environmental organisations.

- **Outcome:** Establishes a benchmark for tracking biodiversity changes over time.

20.2.2 Integrating Biodiversity Into Environmental Impact Assessments (EIAs)

Biodiversity considerations should be incorporated into the business's regular environmental impact assessments (EIAs). An EIA evaluates how a business's operations affect the environment, including the potential impacts on local ecosystems, species, and natural resources. By integrating biodiversity into the EIA process, businesses can make informed decisions about site selection, resource extraction, or land use that minimize harm to ecosystems.

- **Actionable Practice:** Include biodiversity-specific indicators in the EIA process, such as the number of endangered species in the area or the potential disruption to critical habitats.

- **Outcome:** Identifies potential biodiversity risks before they become significant problems.

20.2.3 Continuous Monitoring and Reporting

Ongoing monitoring allows businesses to track changes in biodiversity over time. This can be done through regular field surveys, remote sensing technologies (e.g., satellite imagery), or environmental audits. Monitoring helps ensure that biodiversity goals are being met and that any negative impacts are addressed promptly.

- **Actionable Practice:** Set up a regular monitoring schedule to measure biodiversity indicators, including species populations, ecosystem health, and habitat quality.

- **Outcome:** Provides continuous data for informed decision-making and reporting.

20.2.4 Collaboration with External Experts and Organisations

To accurately measure biodiversity and understand its broader impact, businesses should collaborate with environmental experts, conservation organisations, and researchers. These experts can help design effective measurement strategies, analyse data, and interpret results to ensure the business's efforts are impactful.

- **Actionable Practice:** Partner with NGOs, universities, or environmental consultants specializing in biodiversity monitoring and impact analysis.
- **Outcome:** Ensures the accuracy and credibility of biodiversity measurements.

20.3 Reporting Biodiversity Performance

20.3.1 Transparent and Standardised Reporting

Once biodiversity metrics are collected, businesses need to report their findings in a transparent and consistent manner. Standardised frameworks like the Global Reporting Initiative (GRI) or the Integrated Reporting Framework (IR) offer guidelines on how businesses can disclose their environmental performance, including biodiversity impacts. These reports should be accessible to all stakeholders, including investors, regulators, and customers, to foster accountability.

- **Actionable Practice:** Follow internationally recognised reporting frameworks and disclose biodiversity data regularly in annual sustainability reports or standalone biodiversity reports.
- **Outcome:** Increases transparency and allows stakeholders to assess the business's commitment to sustainability.

20.3.2 Engaging Stakeholders Through Biodiversity Reporting

Effective reporting should not only share data but also engage stakeholders by explaining the steps the business is taking to address biodiversity impacts. Providing context, setting goals, and outlining challenges demonstrates that the company is actively working toward solutions.

- **Actionable Practice:** Include qualitative information, such as the business's biodiversity goals, challenges, and the actions being taken to address biodiversity risks and opportunities.

- **Outcome:** Builds trust with stakeholders and highlights the company's efforts to protect biodiversity.

20.3.3 Setting Clear Biodiversity Goals and Targets

To ensure the effectiveness of biodiversity efforts, businesses should set clear, measurable biodiversity targets aligned with global frameworks like the UN Sustainable Development Goals (SDGs) and the Convention on Biological Diversity (CBD). These targets should be ambitious yet achievable and include clear timelines for achieving progress.

- **Actionable Practice:** Establish specific, time-bound biodiversity targets, such as increasing species populations, reducing deforestation, or restoring degraded ecosystems.

- **Outcome:** Provides a clear focus for biodiversity efforts and enables progress tracking.

20.4 Conclusion: The Future of Biodiversity Measurement and Reporting

Measuring and reporting biodiversity is a complex but essential part of any company's sustainability efforts. By establishing effective measurement strategies, setting clear goals, and reporting progress transparently, businesses can ensure that they contribute positively to the protection of biodiversity while maintaining accountability with stakeholders. The increasing demand for sustainability and biodiversity conservation will continue to shape the landscape of corporate responsibility, and businesses that lead in this area will be better positioned for long-term success.

As businesses continue to Prioritise biodiversity, Chapter 21 will delve into the role of technology in biodiversity monitoring and the future of sustainability tools.

Chapter 21: The Role of Technology in Biodiversity Monitoring and Sustainability Tools

As we continue our journey towards more sustainable business practices, it becomes clear that technology plays a pivotal role in driving progress. In the field of biodiversity conservation, advancements in technology offer powerful tools to monitor ecosystems, track species, and predict environmental changes. These innovations not only enhance our understanding of biodiversity but also help businesses improve their sustainability practices and align more effectively with environmental goals.

In this chapter, we will explore how technology is transforming biodiversity monitoring and how businesses can leverage these tools to improve their environmental performance.

21.1 The Importance of Technology in Biodiversity Monitoring

21.1.1 Why Technology Matters for Biodiversity Conservation

Monitoring biodiversity is a complex task, especially when it comes to tracking vast ecosystems and numerous species across large geographical areas. Traditional methods, such as field surveys and manual data collection, while effective, are often time-consuming, costly, and limited in scope. With the advent of new technologies, businesses now have the ability to monitor biodiversity on a much larger scale and with greater accuracy.

Technologies such as satellite imagery, drones, remote sensing, and artificial intelligence (AI) are helping businesses collect real-time data, process vast amounts of information, and make informed decisions. These tools not only improve efficiency but also provide businesses with the ability to track biodiversity trends, assess environmental risks, and engage stakeholders in more meaningful ways.

- **Actionable Practice:** Implement cutting-edge technologies, such as drones or AI-powered analytics, to monitor biodiversity and environmental changes in real-time.
- **Outcome:** Provides a more accurate, scalable, and efficient approach to biodiversity monitoring, allowing businesses to address challenges proactively.

21.1.2 Key Technologies for Biodiversity Monitoring

Some of the most transformative technologies for biodiversity monitoring include:

- **Remote Sensing and Satellite Imagery:** These tools allow businesses to monitor large and inaccessible areas of land, detect land-use changes, and observe habitat degradation. Satellite imagery can also provide data on forest cover, water quality, and overall ecosystem health.

- **Drones and UAVs (Unmanned Aerial Vehicles):** Drones are increasingly used to capture high-resolution images and video of ecosystems, track wildlife populations, and monitor vegetation health. Drones are particularly useful in hard-to-reach areas, such as forests, wetlands, and coastal zones.

- **AI and Machine Learning:** AI-powered tools can analyse vast amounts of data, from satellite images to camera trap images, to identify species, track migration patterns, and assess habitat quality. Machine learning algorithms can also predict environmental risks, such as biodiversity loss or the impact of climate change on ecosystems.

- **Environmental DNA (eDNA) Analysis:** This innovative technology allows scientists to detect traces of DNA left behind by organisms in the environment, such as water, soil, or air. By collecting and analysing eDNA, businesses can monitor species presence, biodiversity changes, and even detect invasive species.

- **IoT (Internet of Things) and Sensors:** IoT devices and environmental sensors can be deployed to track environmental conditions such as soil moisture, water quality, temperature, and air pollution. These devices provide real-time data on the health of ecosystems and the impact of business activities.

- **Actionable Practice:** Invest in AI, remote sensing tools, and drones to gather data on biodiversity health and ecosystems over time.

- **Outcome:** Enhances the accuracy of data collection and improves the ability to identify trends, risks, and opportunities in biodiversity management.

21.2 How Businesses Can Use Technology to Improve Biodiversity Performance

21.2.1 Real-Time Data Collection and Analysis

With the ability to collect real-time data, businesses can make more informed decisions faster. For instance, remote sensing technologies provide up-to-date information about the health of habitats or ecosystems, which can be integrated into the business's environmental risk assessments. By continuously monitoring biodiversity, businesses can quickly identify problems and adapt strategies to reduce their impact.

- **Actionable Practice:** Use real-time data from sensors and drones to monitor water bodies, forests, and wildlife, allowing businesses to act swiftly when threats to biodiversity are identified.
- **Outcome:** Reduces the risk of damage to ecosystems by enabling early detection of issues like pollution, habitat destruction, or invasive species.

21.2.2 Biodiversity Prediction and Risk Management

AI and machine learning algorithms can help businesses predict future biodiversity risks by analysing past and present data. For example, AI models can forecast the impact of climate change on specific species or ecosystems, helping businesses make more informed decisions about land use, resource extraction, or conservation efforts.

- **Actionable Practice:** Implement AI tools to predict the future effects of business activities on biodiversity, helping businesses design strategies to mitigate potential risks.
- **Outcome:** Enhances climate resilience and long-term sustainability by preparing for future biodiversity challenges.

21.2.3 Engaging Stakeholders Through Technology

Technology also allows businesses to communicate biodiversity progress to stakeholders more effectively. By using interactive maps, data dashboards, and visualizations, companies can share insights into their biodiversity performance with investors, customers, and the public.

- **Actionable Practice:** Create interactive dashboards or digital platforms to share biodiversity data and sustainability progress with stakeholders.
- **Outcome:** Increases transparency, strengthens stakeholder trust, and encourages greater engagement in biodiversity initiatives.

21.3 Case Studies of Technology-Driven Biodiversity Monitoring

21.3.1 Case Study 1: Drones in Forestry Conservation

A forestry company in the Amazon rainforest has partnered with conservation NGOs to deploy drones for monitoring deforestation. Using high-resolution aerial images captured by drones, the company is able to track changes in forest cover in real-time, pinpoint areas at risk of illegal logging, and assess the effectiveness of their conservation efforts.

- **Outcome:** This technology has significantly improved the company's ability to protect biodiversity by detecting illegal activities faster and taking corrective actions immediately.

21.3.2 Case Study 2: AI in Species Identification

A leading agricultural business has integrated AI technology into its biodiversity monitoring systems to identify and track species in local ecosystems. By analysing camera trap images, AI algorithms are able to automatically identify different species, including endangered ones, in the area surrounding the business's facilities.

- **Outcome:** This allows the company to monitor wildlife populations, understand their movement patterns, and take appropriate actions to protect these species, ensuring that their operations do not interfere with critical habitats.

21.4 The Future of Technology in Biodiversity Monitoring

21.4.1 Expanding the Role of Technology

As technology continues to evolve, its role in biodiversity monitoring will only grow. Advances in satellite capabilities, AI, and sensors will allow businesses to monitor biodiversity on a global scale, providing a more accurate picture of the health of ecosystems and enabling more effective conservation actions.

21.4.2 Blockchain for Transparent Reporting

Blockchain technology is being explored as a means to create transparent, verifiable records of biodiversity conservation efforts. Blockchain could be used to track the progress of biodiversity projects, document carbon offset transactions, and verify sustainability claims, ensuring that companies are held accountable for their actions.

21.5 Conclusion: Harnessing Technology for Sustainability and Biodiversity

The integration of technology in biodiversity monitoring presents businesses with opportunities to make more informed decisions, improve sustainability practices, and engage stakeholders. From AI-powered analytics to remote sensing technologies, businesses now have access to a wealth of tools that can enhance their environmental performance and biodiversity conservation efforts.

By embracing these technologies, businesses not only contribute to protecting the planet's biodiversity but also gain a competitive advantage in an increasingly environmentally-conscious market. As businesses look to the future, the combination of technology and sustainability will be a driving force in achieving both economic success and environmental stewardship.

Chapter 22: Integrating First Nations Knowledge in Biodiversity Conservation

Incorporating traditional knowledge from First Nations peoples is a powerful and often overlooked tool in biodiversity conservation. Indigenous communities have long understood the intricate relationships between land, water, and wildlife, possessing a deep knowledge of ecosystems passed down through generations. As the world increasingly recognises the importance of biodiversity preservation, it becomes clear that integrating First Nations knowledge alongside modern scientific approaches can significantly enhance conservation efforts.

This chapter focuses on the importance of integrating First Nations knowledge into biodiversity conservation strategies, with a particular focus on how businesses can engage with Indigenous communities and incorporate traditional practices in sustainable management.

22.1 The Value of First Nations Knowledge in Biodiversity Conservation

22.1.1 Understanding the Depth of Traditional Ecological Knowledge (TEK)

Traditional Ecological Knowledge (TEK) refers to the understanding Indigenous peoples have developed about their natural environment over thousands of years. This knowledge includes practices related to land and resource management, species identification, ecological health, and climate patterns. TEK often involves an intimate understanding of how ecosystems function and the importance of maintaining balance within these systems.

Indigenous knowledge systems are grounded in a holistic view of the environment. First Nations communities traditionally viewed humans not as separate from nature, but as part of it, with an inherent responsibility to care for the land, water, and creatures within their territory.

- **Actionable Practice:** Engage with First Nations communities to access their traditional ecological knowledge and understand local ecosystems in a more integrated, respectful way.

- **Outcome:** Enables businesses to design more sustainable practices that respect local knowledge and enhance biodiversity conservation.

22.1.2 Bridging the Gap Between Western Science and Traditional Knowledge

Historically, Western scientific approaches and Indigenous knowledge have been viewed as separate or even contradictory. However, increasing recognition of the value of both perspectives is leading to a more collaborative approach to conservation. Integrating Western scientific research with Indigenous wisdom allows for a more comprehensive understanding of ecosystems and biodiversity.

For example, many Indigenous practices, such as controlled burning in Australian bushlands or selective harvesting of plants, have proven to be effective in maintaining biodiversity. These practices, when combined with modern scientific understanding, can provide more sustainable management solutions.

- **Actionable Practice:** Create partnerships between businesses, scientists, and First Nations communities to combine traditional knowledge with modern conservation methods.
- **Outcome:** Results in more effective biodiversity management strategies that are culturally sensitive and ecologically sustainable.

22.2 Best Practices for Integrating First Nations Knowledge in Biodiversity Initiatives

22.2.1 Respecting Indigenous Land and Knowledge Rights

One of the most fundamental aspects of working with First Nations communities is ensuring that their rights are respected. Indigenous peoples hold legal and cultural rights over their lands and resources, and any conservation efforts must align with these rights. This includes obtaining **Free, Prior, and Informed Consent (FPIC)**, which ensures that Indigenous communities are fully informed about any conservation initiatives and that they have the right to give or withhold consent.

Respecting these rights is not only a legal obligation but also an ethical one that forms the foundation for genuine, mutually beneficial partnerships.

- **Actionable Practice:** Before engaging in any conservation projects or research, seek FPIC from First Nations communities and involve them in decision-making processes.

- **Outcome:** Builds trust, strengthens relationships, and ensures that conservation efforts align with the needs and rights of Indigenous peoples.

22.2.2 Collaborating on Land and Resource Management

One of the most effective ways businesses can integrate First Nations knowledge is by collaborating with Indigenous communities in land and resource management. Many First Nations peoples have practiced land stewardship for millennia, developing sustainable practices that can be applied to modern conservation challenges.

Businesses can work with Indigenous communities to:

- **Co-manage Protected Areas**: Collaborating on the management of national parks, nature reserves, and other protected areas ensures that biodiversity is preserved according to traditional knowledge systems and modern conservation science.

- **Implement Sustainable Land Use Practices**: First Nations communities often have sustainable practices for agriculture, forestry, and water management that businesses can adopt to improve their environmental impact.

- **Restore Ecosystems**: Indigenous knowledge of reforestation, fire management, and species regeneration can be integrated into broader restoration programs.

- **Actionable Practice:** Form joint management committees with First Nations groups to co-manage local biodiversity resources and ensure that both traditional and scientific methods are integrated.

- **Outcome:** More effective conservation practices that respect Indigenous stewardship and improve environmental sustainability.

22.2.3 Supporting Indigenous-Led Conservation Projects

Indigenous-led conservation initiatives have proven to be highly effective in preserving biodiversity. By funding and supporting these initiatives, businesses not only help to protect the environment but also empower Indigenous communities. These projects may include wildlife protection, habitat restoration, and climate change mitigation strategies, and they can be a powerful tool for community development.

Businesses can support Indigenous-led conservation efforts by:

- **Providing Funding and Resources**: Financial support is often crucial for the success of Indigenous-led projects. Businesses can allocate funds for projects like wildlife corridors or habitat restoration programs.

- **Providing Technical Assistance**: Some Indigenous groups may need assistance with technology, scientific expertise, or project management skills to implement their conservation projects.

- **Developing Long-Term Partnerships**: Sustainable partnerships with Indigenous communities can help build local capacity, create jobs, and support long-term conservation goals.

- **Actionable Practice:** Partner with Indigenous organisations that focus on conservation, providing funding, resources, or technical expertise.

- **Outcome:** Strengthens Indigenous leadership in conservation and ensures long-term environmental protection.

22.3 Case Studies: Successful Integration of First Nations Knowledge

22.3.1 Case Study: The Great Barrier Reef and Indigenous Collaboration

In Australia, the Great Barrier Reef is not only a World Heritage-listed site but also an area of immense cultural significance for the traditional owners of the land. Indigenous communities in the region have been working closely with conservation groups and government agencies to protect the Reef. By integrating traditional knowledge, such as coral reef restoration techniques, with scientific research, these communities have been successful in helping mitigate the impact of climate change and human activity on the Reef.

- **Outcome:** The collaboration has led to better management practices, an improved understanding of the Reef's ecosystems, and greater involvement of Indigenous communities in its preservation.

22.3.2 Case Study: Firestick Alliance and Cultural Burning

The Firestick Alliance, an Indigenous-led organization, promotes the use of traditional fire management techniques to prevent bushfires and protect biodiversity. By using **cultural burning** techniques, First Nations groups manage landscapes to reduce fuel loads and promote biodiversity, while minimizing the risk of uncontrolled wildfires. This practice has gained recognition from environmental groups and government agencies.

- **Outcome:** Cultural burning has been shown to improve ecosystem health, reduce wildfire risks, and restore biodiversity in areas of Australia prone to bushfires.

22.4 Conclusion: Bridging the Gap Between Modern Conservation and Traditional Knowledge

Integrating First Nations knowledge into biodiversity conservation is not just an ethical obligation; it is a strategic necessity. First Nations communities have a profound understanding of the ecosystems they inhabit and have developed sustainable practices that businesses and governments can learn from. By working together, businesses can help protect the environment, preserve cultural heritage, and create more sustainable and equitable futures for all.

Incorporating Indigenous perspectives into sustainability efforts leads to more comprehensive, effective, and culturally respectful conservation strategies. As businesses continue to explore new ways to reduce their environmental impact, integrating traditional knowledge will be key to fostering long-term sustainability.

In the next chapter, we will explore how businesses can develop strategies to ensure they are supporting both the environmental and social aspects of the UN's Sustainable Development Goals, with a particular focus on inclusivity and community-driven change.

Chapter 23: Contributing to the Sustainable Development Goals (SDGs) Through ESG Strategies

As businesses continue to embrace sustainability, aligning operations with the **United Nations' Sustainable Development Goals (SDGs)** has become an essential part of their corporate strategies. The SDGs represent a global blueprint for achieving a better and more sustainable future for all, addressing challenges such as poverty, inequality, environmental degradation, and peace. Businesses, particularly those in Australia, can play a pivotal role in advancing these goals by integrating them into their environmental, social, and governance (ESG) frameworks.

This final chapter of the book will explore how businesses can contribute to the SDGs, focusing on the synergy between First Nations sustainability practices and broader corporate ESG strategies. We will provide guidance on how companies can set actionable goals, track their progress, and ensure they make a meaningful impact on sustainable development both locally and globally.

23.1 Understanding the SDGs and Their Importance to Business

The 17 Sustainable Development Goals (SDGs) were adopted by the United Nations in 2015 as part of the **2030 Agenda for Sustainable Development**. These goals encompass a broad range of issues, from environmental sustainability and climate action to health, education, gender equality, and social justice. As businesses increasingly recognise their responsibility in supporting these global goals, integrating SDGs into their operational strategies is no longer optional—it is a fundamental expectation.

The SDGs are not only about corporate responsibility—they present significant opportunities for growth, innovation, and value creation. Companies that align their operations with the SDGs can access new markets, build stronger relationships with stakeholders, and improve their sustainability performance.

- **Actionable Practice:** Review the SDGs and identify which goals align most closely with your business's values, activities, and capabilities.

- **Outcome:** Aligning business activities with the SDGs leads to more robust corporate strategies, enhanced reputation, and improved operational performance.

23.2 Integrating the SDGs into ESG Strategies

Integrating the SDGs into ESG strategies involves aligning business practices with specific SDGs and developing frameworks to track progress. Businesses should focus on tangible actions that address the environmental, social, and governance pillars of sustainability, while also considering the impact on local communities, especially First Nations communities in Australia.

23.2.1 Environmental Responsibility: Promoting Climate Action and Biodiversity Preservation

For businesses committed to environmental sustainability, SDGs 13 (Climate Action), 14 (Life Below Water), and 15 (Life on Land) are of particular importance. Aligning with these goals requires proactive efforts to reduce environmental footprints, conserve biodiversity, and mitigate climate-related risks.

- **Actionable Practice:** Establish science-based emission reduction targets, commit to renewable energy sources, and integrate conservation practices such as sustainable land use and biodiversity protection into business strategies.
- **Outcome:** These actions not only align with climate action goals but also enhance the organisation's credibility and long-term environmental stewardship.

23.2.2 Social Responsibility: Advancing Social Justice and Community Empowerment

Socially, SDGs 1 (No Poverty), 3 (Good Health and Well-being), 5 (Gender Equality), 10 (Reduced Inequalities), and 11 (Sustainable Cities and Communities) are pivotal. Businesses should invest in programs that directly benefit underrepresented groups, such as First Nations communities, as well as other marginalised sectors. These programs should focus on reducing poverty, improving access to education and healthcare, and advancing gender equality.

- **Actionable Practice:** Develop partnerships with First Nations organisations, implement local community programs, and ensure fair wages and working conditions that align with SDG 8 (Decent Work and Economic Growth).

- **Outcome:** These efforts create positive social impacts while also fostering greater inclusion, diversity, and equity within the organization and the wider community.

23.2.3 Governance Excellence: Promoting Transparency, Peace, and Strong Institutions

Good governance is a critical element of the SDGs, particularly SDGs 16 (Peace, Justice, and Strong Institutions) and 17 (Partnerships for the Goals). To contribute to these goals, businesses must ensure ethical conduct, transparency, and accountability in all operations.

- **Actionable Practice:** Implement anti-corruption policies, encourage stakeholder engagement, and ensure your governance structures are inclusive and accountable. Ensure your reporting is transparent and aligns with frameworks such as the **Global Reporting Initiative (GRI)** or the **Task Force on Climate-related Financial Disclosures (TCFD)**.
- **Outcome:** Improved governance practices help create stronger relationships with stakeholders, align the company with ethical standards, and contribute to peace and justice both within and outside the organization.

23.3 First Nations Partnerships and Contributions to the SDGs

A vital part of achieving the SDGs in Australia involves empowering **First Nations communities**. By integrating traditional knowledge, respecting land rights, and supporting First Nations-led sustainability initiatives, businesses can significantly contribute to the achievement of the SDGs.

23.3.1 SDGs 1 (No Poverty) and 10 (Reduced Inequalities)

Businesses can help reduce poverty and inequality by providing employment opportunities for Indigenous people, supporting Indigenous businesses, and funding programs that enhance education and skill development in Indigenous communities. These efforts can directly support SDGs 1 and 10.

- **Actionable Practice:** Develop initiatives that Prioritise the hiring of Indigenous peoples, support Indigenous-owned businesses, and invest in education and community capacity-building.

- **Outcome:** These actions provide long-term economic opportunities for Indigenous communities and contribute to reducing inequality and poverty.

23.3.2 SDG 15 (Life on Land) and SDG 13 (Climate Action)

First Nations communities have valuable insights into land stewardship and environmental conservation. By partnering with Indigenous groups on conservation projects, businesses can help restore ecosystems and protect biodiversity, contributing to SDGs 13 and 15.

- **Actionable Practice:** Partner with First Nations communities to implement traditional ecological practices like fire-stick alliance programs, sustainable land use, and bush regeneration.

- **Outcome:** These collaborations can help mitigate climate risks, protect biodiversity, and restore ecosystems.

23.4 Tracking and Reporting SDG Contributions

As businesses integrate SDGs into their strategies, they must establish systems to track progress and demonstrate accountability. Regular reporting helps businesses show how their activities are aligned with the SDGs and provides stakeholders with transparent information on progress.

23.4.1 Creating Key Performance Indicators (KPIs) for SDGs

To effectively track contributions to the SDGs, businesses should create KPIs that measure the impact of their sustainability initiatives. These KPIs should be aligned with the specific SDGs the company is prioritising, and they should be reviewed periodically to ensure that the goals are being met.

- **Actionable Practice:** Develop KPIs for each SDG your business focuses on, such as carbon emissions reduction for SDG 13, water use reduction for SDG 6, or community engagement for SDG 10.

- **Outcome:** Clear KPIs provide tangible benchmarks for assessing progress and allow businesses to make necessary adjustments to stay on track.

23.4.2 Reporting Progress Through Transparent Frameworks

In addition to tracking KPIs, businesses should report their progress using internationally recognised frameworks such as **GRI** or **TCFD**. These frameworks ensure that businesses are reporting their sustainability efforts in a standardised, transparent way, which builds trust with stakeholders.

- **Actionable Practice:** Use GRI, TCFD, or other recognised frameworks to disclose your business's sustainability efforts and SDG contributions.
- **Outcome:** Transparent reporting helps build stakeholder trust, demonstrates accountability, and showcases the business's commitment to sustainability.

23.5 Conclusion: A Path Toward Sustainable and Inclusive Growth

Incorporating the SDGs into business strategies is no longer optional—it is a necessity for companies that aim to thrive in an increasingly sustainable world. The goals set forth by the United Nations offer businesses an opportunity to make a positive, lasting impact on the world, both socially and environmentally.

By aligning ESG strategies with the SDGs and working alongside First Nations communities, businesses can help address some of the most pressing global challenges. Whether it's protecting biodiversity, fostering economic opportunities, or advancing social justice, businesses have the power to drive transformative change.

This book has highlighted how businesses can integrate First Nations sustainability practices, environmental stewardship, and inclusive growth into their ESG strategies. As we move toward a more sustainable future, businesses have an essential role in shaping a world where people, planet, and profit can coexist in harmony.

In conclusion, businesses that embrace the SDGs as a core part of their operations will not only contribute to global sustainability but also build a stronger, more resilient, and equitable future for all.

Conclusion:

The journey towards a truly sustainable business model is not without its challenges. But as we have explored throughout this book, the benefits of embedding environmental, social, and governance (ESG) principles into your operations are profound. By embracing biodiversity conservation, engaging with Indigenous communities, and adopting sustainable practices, businesses can not only contribute to the achievement of the United Nations' Sustainable Development Goals but also foster lasting positive change for future generations.

We have seen that collaboration—whether through integrating traditional knowledge, supporting local conservation efforts, or promoting responsible consumption—holds the key to unlocking the full potential of businesses committed to sustainability. The role of First Nations in Australia as the original custodians of the land cannot be overstated, and businesses that align with their wisdom and respect their rights will lead the charge in the green economy.

As we conclude, the message is clear: sustainable business practices are not just a moral imperative—they are a pathway to long-term success. The time to act is now, and the responsibility lies with each of us to make a meaningful impact. By working in partnership with First Nations communities, supporting biodiversity, and fostering ethical governance, businesses can not only contribute to a thriving planet but also create a better, more equitable future for all.

The future is green, and it is one that we can shape together. Let us rise to the challenge, and together, we will build a world that future generations will be proud to inherit.

www.ingramcontent.com/pod-product-compliance
Lightning Source LLC
Chambersburg PA
CBHW071126240526
45465CB00024B/1403